NO SWANK

Other books by
Sherwood Anderson

NO SWANK

Sherwood Anderson

PAUL P. APPEL, *Publisher*

MAMARONECK, N.Y.

1970

to

Laura Lou Copenhaver

in appreciation

A NOTE

Bits from this book have been published in
The New Republic, Today, The Virginia Quarterly Review, The American Spectator and
in the Virginia country newspapers—The
Marion *Democrat* and The Smyth County *News*

THIS LIFE YOU LIVE,
the impression you get of life going on in others . . .

Nothing comes to you rounded and whole.

Why am I so alive to impressions today and so dead to them tomorrow.

I cannot tell why it is so.

There is this phase, of some fellow of mine, coming to me at a certain moment. It is foolish to think that it is all of him. It may stay with me while I live but it would be absurd to think that this glance, this flash of light out of darkness . . . myself at the moment gathering impressions swiftly, storing them away . . . this I know is not, cannot be, a rounded picture of this other man . . .

Or for that matter of a woman, a field, a river, a town.

Excuse it, my fellow humans.

If any of you of whom I here write are alive, my fellows, perhaps even friends, do not think that I am pretending to give a complete or even a just picture of you.

SHERWOOD ANDERSON

CONTENTS

MEETING
RING LARDNER

A LONG, SOLEMN-faced man. The face was wonderful. It was a mask. All the time, when you were with him, you kept wondering . . . "what is going on back there?"

I was in New Orleans, at the Mardi Gras time, and he telephoned. I had long admired but had never seen the man. He had come to New Orleans for the Mardi Gras, accompanied by his friend Grantland Rice, and it developed that Rice had been afraid that Ring, whom he admired with something like adoration, would not get the attention he deserved. He had got Ring in up to his neck and the voice on the 'phone was a pleading one. "Please, Sherwood," it said, "you do not know me, you have never seen me, you do not even know that you have invited me to dinner tonight?"

"Yes," I said, "I know. I even know where." There was a little place, upstairs, down in the French quarter. It had just been opened by a Frenchman who had been, until a few months before, the chef at Antoine's. "It is

1

a little place and dark," I said. "We could get eight or ten into the room.

"Good wine. Good food," I said, and "O. K.," he said. "I'll bring my wife and Mr. Fixit and his wife. I hope it is very dark and very dirty. If it isn't very dirty have them shovel a little dirt into the place. I'll be there."

And so we dined and Ring talked. I think the mask dropped away for that evening. The man was surrounded by a little halo of something like worship. It was in the eyes of the women in the room, in the men's eyes. I had hurried down in the late morning to see the French chef. "What," he said, "Ring Lardner? You wait. You'll see."

So he too knew about Ring, had a feeling about him. During the dinner and afterwards, over the wine, he kept tiptoeing down a little dark hallway. He put his head in at the door and made a sign to me and I slid out to him. "Is it all right? Does he like it? Does he like the wine?" He slipped another bottle into my hand. "Try this one on him."

There was something loose and free in the little room. How shall I describe it? It was Ring. What we all felt for him was warm affection. I had never known any one just like him in writing in America. He awoke a certain feeling. You wanted him not to be hurt, perhaps to have some freedom he did not have. There was a feeling . . . "if any one hurts this man I'd like to punch him on the jaw." Almost always, when one of your friends gets kicked down stairs, you're glad. It is a nasty fact, but it is a truth.

I dare say that the tragedy of Ring Lardner . . . that gorgeous talent of his so often smeared . . . is our common tragedy, the tragedy of every creative man, big or little, in our day. No one of us escapes it. How can he?

Just the same, Ring Lardner did often escape. He had a marvelous technique. He could always get behind the mask, and then, too, he must always have had a great deal of what he was getting that night at the dinner, that is to say, warm affection from many people. We poured it over him as we poured the wine down our throats. We loved him. I cannot help thinking it was a rare and a rich evening in his life. He laughed. He talked. He drank the wine. He told stories. It was a good evening for him. It was something more than that for the rest of us. Two years later I was in the same little restaurant and the chef, that fat Frenchman, came to my table. I was alone and he brought a bottle of wine. He had come in from the kitchen and had on his white apron. He stood beside my table and poured wine for us both. "To that man you brought here that time . . . to Ring Lardner," he said, lifting his glass. . . .

And there was another evening two days later. He and Grantland Rice must have been going it hard. Any number of people would have been wanting to meet Ring, to entertain him. He was at the top of his fame then. I don't blame them. He could make a party go, put life and fun into it. Both the high- and the low-brows loved him. He 'phoned me on his way from one party to another. I was to come and get him. The party to which he was bound was in a swell house in a swell part of town.

When I arrived there was a swarm of people and Ring was busy. He was putting on a show. He sat in the middle of a big room at a piano and they were all gathered about him and he was singing and making them sing with him. He sang "Two Little Girls in Blue" . . . "Just Tell Her that You Saw Me and that I Was Looking Well" . . . "There'll Be a Hot Time in the Old Town Tonight," and several others. He made them sing. There were drinks aplenty. A little river of liquor flowed through the room.

There was the expensive furniture, and paintings on the walls. In New Orleans the rich go in for heavily paneled walls, heavy uncomfortable French furniture.

The people were crowded in close about Ring, who sat at the piano wearing his mask. He could look at a man or woman with strangely impersonal eyes. "Sing," he said and the person so looked at sang. They were the sort of people you see photographs of in the Sunday newspapers, on the society pages. We writers, painters, *etc.*, sweat our heads off trying to do, now and then, a little thing that is worth doing and then some dame . . . enough money in that gown on her back to give one of us a half year's leisure. At that it doesn't cover her back much. Hail revolution!

There were heavy-faced rich men, young male society swells, horsey men, down from New York, for the races, and women . . . women and more women.

It was quite a long time before Ring saw me that night but when he did he made for me, the singing having stopped abruptly . . . he had them going all right . . . they had been throwing their heads back, drinking the liquor and stepping into it. He pushed me through them, brushing them aside. Now and then he stopped to introduce me to a man or woman. The mask on his face was well adjusted. He introduced me as an author, his fellow author, the author of "The Great Gadsby" . . . "The Confessions of a Young Man" . . . "Tess of the d'Urbervilles" . . . the man who wrote "Moby Dick."

He kept pressing me on and on through the crowd and we got into a hallway. He pointed to a door. "It's what they call 'the butler's pantry,'" he said. "I don't believe there is any one in there. They are taking drinks about.

"Get three or four bottles of their best stuff," he said, "and we'll get out." He told me where to meet him outside.

I did what he told me to do. I went outside and waited. I got a taxi and made it pull in to the curb. I put the bottles on the floor. I had got six quarts. It looked to me like pretty good stuff.

And then, when he came, he came in the host's car and our host was with him. He was a small man and pale and right away I knew he was a banker. The stuff was in the taxi and I was walking up and down. It was a tough break for us.

I got into the cab for a moment and fixed myself as best I could. Luckily I had on an overcoat. Then I crawled into the back seat of that car. I rattled a good deal but Ring, on the front seat with that man, that little pale banker, didn't seem to mind. He was wearing the mask. He looked at me and growled. "Sit still, Sherwood," he said. "Don't rattle so much."

I tried not to rattle but I had to get out of the car again when we got to his hotel. I crept out and got into the hotel entrance. I got to where I could see without being seen. Ring stood on the sidewalk.

Our host had got out of his car. It was a Rolls-Royce. He was doing his own driving. "Your friend, your fellow author—where is he?" he said to Ring, looking about. He seemed extraordinarily small and pale, standing there before Ring. It was like a big dog and a little dog and the little dog was wagging his tail. He didn't care a hang about the liquor we had got. He knew we were going somewhere to sit and drink and talk quietly and I think he wanted to come along, but he was too polite to ask and I think also that Ring was, for a moment, tempted to ask him to come.

Ring was looking down at the man. I could see it all. There was an overhead light shining on them. I saw something happen. Ring had been wearing his mask all evening, but, for a moment, it dropped. He started to ask the man to come with us but changed his mind. I saw his lips tremble. I know what happened. He wanted to ask the man to come along but was afraid I wouldn't like it and so he said nothing but stood there, looking down at the man, his lips trembling. This was a different Ring Lardner from the one I had seen in the room with all those people.

This one was a shy man and so was the little banker. The two men stood like that, looking hard at each other and then, as by a common impulse, they both began to laugh. They laughed like two young boys, or for that matter like two girls, and then the banker ran quickly and got into his car and drove away but as he did so he took a shot back at Ring. "I hope your friend got plenty of good stuff . . . I hope he got enough," he said, but Ring was not looking. He was a man whose habit it was to wear a mask, and it had slipped off and at the moment I was like a man standing in the dressing room of a theater and watching an actor at work on his make-up. I saw him put the mask back on his face and he wore it for the rest of the evening.

DEATH
ON A WINTER DAY

A GRAY AND LEAN man, Leon Bazalgette. He had his headquarters, when I knew him, at 59 Rue Renneguin, on the left bank in Paris. It must have been some eight or ten years ago when I met him first.

As a writer I was unknown to the French then, and am comparatively unknown to them still. In the arts the French do not readily take in outsiders. "We have our own writers and painters. Why should we bother with others?"

However, Leon Bazalgette knew of my scribbling. He knew of writers in South American countries, of writers from our own Pacific Coast, from the far East. The man was a cosmopolitan. He was the first man of his kind I had ever known.

He had come to my little left bank hotel to seek me out, this man with the gray, pallid skin and the kind eyes. He had read some of my tales of my Ohio country. "A blessing on you for making me feel your own land

9

and people," he said. "I am glad you do not try to write like a European."

So we sat in the little hotel room and talked for two or three hours. He was at that time the editor of a well-known literary magazine in Paris—a literatus, a lover of the written word, a European man of culture. I had never before met such a one.

Bazalgette was, I dare say, a comparatively poor man. Most European men of letters are. The French do not have great magazines, with huge prices for their popular writers, as do we. He had, however, a little Normandy farm with a river running through it, and he talked to me of the farm. He wanted me to go there with him and I am sorry now that I didn't.

We talked in my hotel room and in sidewalk cafés, over bottles of light, delicate French wine, of art and of the places we had seen and of writers we had known. He told me of the French writers I did not know and could not know because I had no French and they had no English, what they were like, what sort of men they were.

Five years passed before I was again in Paris and again saw him.

I was in my hotel room, sick with the flu, when he came up a narrow stairs and knocked at the door.

"Who is there?"

"Leon Bazalgette."

"But you must not come in. I have been looking forward to seeing you. To see and talk with you again was
the chief reason I wanted to return to Paris, but you are
no longer a young man and must not be exposed to this
disease."

There was a laugh in the hallway and my door was
pushed open. "It is because you are a man I respect and
love that I must come in.

"Is a mere disease to stand between us? To live is to
see often the men and women you love and to talk with
them," he said, coming into the room and taking a chair
near my bed. How gray and gentle he looked sitting
there in the afternoon light! "There never was such another gentleman," I thought, looking at him.

"As for disease and death," he said, "what of such
things? We must, all of us, die in our time. The time is
a matter for the gods. While he lives a man must go to
see his men friends and talk to them of art. If he loves
a woman he must make love to her."

For two or three hours we talked and then he went
away. I did not stay in Paris. I was ill and it was winter.
The skies were gray and cold as they are this morning as
I sit writing of my friend.

Later Bazalgette published a book of mine, translated
into the French. He himself translated some of the tales.
He was the Frenchman who did most, in his day, to

make the French know the writers of other countries. The poems of our Walt Whitman were translated by him.

He used often to write me long, charming letters from his little Normandy farm and now, this morning, I have a letter from a friend.

The letter says he is dead. The thought sends a sharp feeling of dread through my frame. Thinking of Bazal- gette dead, the day becomes like the skies, cold and forbidding. I think of many people seen and loved that I shall never again see. I am glad I am here in America, this winter of Bazalgette's death, rather than in Paris. I am thinking that for me Paris will not again be Paris without Leon Bazalgette.

THE
DREISER

THE DREISER IS A BIG
man. There is something burly, impulsive, crude and
tender. When he comes into a room where you are sitting with others it is like a freight engine making its
way slowly and majestically through railroad yards.
There is something else—a kind of natural majesty.
Once, in speaking of him, I compared him to a fine
horse. "He would be a stallion, a Norman Percheron," I
said. Some one present objected. "You are not being
very flattering to your friend." I looked about the room
in which we were sitting. What small picayune things
all in the room suddenly seemed!

He will shock you by the brutality of his utterances,
will beat you down. He swears, doubles his fists. "You
are talking like a damn fool," he shouts. Very likely
you are.

Let us say the conversation is turned upon Soviet Russia.
There may be a dozen people present who are experts
on the subject. It makes no difference to the Dreiser. He

shouts, quoting his facts and figures. He is the master and all the others in the room are children.

Or it is of one of our American masters of finance of whom he speaks. The Dreiser does not mince words. "He is a damn crook. He has stolen so and so many millions of dollars." There is a statistician present. "Aha! You see the Dreiser is inaccurate. He does not get his facts straight. You heard him, did you not? He said the man stole fifteen millions of dollars. It is not correct. How can you trust such a man? He only stole twelve."

The Dreiser has made an impatient movement with his hand.

"Now you listen to me. It is I who am telling you this."

The Dreiser is physically a very strong man. All of this nonsense about his impotence—his own declaration of impotence after the toothpick incident in Harlan, Kentucky . . . what nonsense! He is one of the most potent of American men.

He is essentially tender. There he is on the 'phone. His voice is rough and commanding. On the evening before he has been somewhere with a group of people.

In the group there was a man he and you both know. You have not seen the man for a long time.

The Dreiser is on the 'phone. "I was at Fred's house last night. Tom was there. I want you to go and see Tom."

So there it is. You get a picture of him on the evening before at Fred's house. He was thundering away. "I'm telling you," he was shouting.

But at the same time the Dreiser, this man outwardly so rough, so apparently unaware of others, had been terribly aware. Our mutual acquaintance, Tom, was in the room and as he thundered away, the Dreiser was looking at Tom.

He had noticed that Tom was despondent, down on his luck. The Dreiser had gone home thinking of Tom. Why, Tom is not one of his closest friends. It does not matter. He will have been down to Tom's place. Now he is on the 'phone. "You go down there," he shouts. "He is in trouble and won't tell what it is. You go there at once."

It is his great tenderness that has saved the Dreiser, that has made him a great man. He is always on the lookout for obscure talent, and often, it is true, over-estimates it. "The poor fellow. Look. He is starving. It must be he can paint."

"But Dreiser . . . it does not follow, you see, just because he is poor."

"Ah, you go to hell. Do as I say. Go talk to the man. Go look at his work."

Although the Dreiser is so often rough, browbeating those about him, he now and then becomes very quiet. You are sitting or walking with him and he begins to talk quietly of some adventure of his own life, and what adventures he has had. Now he is at his best. How quiet he is! He is one of the few men you meet who is always giving out life.

It may be a tale of a man met when he was himself a hack writer, in the office of Street and Smith.

"There was a man there. He was such a wonderful fellow."

He begins telling you of some queer, obscure figure, known intimately at that time in his own life. You look at the Dreiser in amazement. Is this the man you have heard others call a bully, the man who, but an hour ago, was shouting every one down?

For see—now there is a transformation. The Dreiser has become like a shy and very sensitive boy. He is telling you a thousand details in the life of some obscure man he has known, a man met perhaps twenty years earlier and not since. There is in the Dreiser now something terrifically appealing. Looking at him so, you do not wonder that women have loved him, that men who know him well, all love him deeply.

He has the gift. It is rare enough in the world. It is the gift of infinite tenderness, always reaching out to the others.

PRIZE FIGHTERS AND AUTHORS

WHY DO INTELLEC-
tual men, writers, painters, *etc.*, often have such a passion
for prize fighters, or, for that matter, for bull fighters?
A short time ago a great fuss was being made about Mr.
Gene Tunney's mind. He probably hadn't too much. A
working mind leaves its marks on the face. There was
nothing particularly sensitive about Mr. Tunney's face.
It was not the face of a bruiser nor yet the face of a
thinker. On the whole, it was a placid face. Mr. Dempsey,
when champion, was more popular. He was more a
creature of impulse. I saw him once and immediately
took to him. We were in the studio of a New York photographer. He took me into a corner of the room. "You
are a writer, eh?" "Yes," I said.

He told me that he had been acting in the movies. "I
hate it," he said. He made no pretense of having a mind,
but I felt at once that he had one, and a good one too.
"I enjoy fighting," he said. He meant that he enjoyed
the rush of it, the plunge, the excitement. He was no
cold, calculating fellow—this Dempsey.

Before a fight the man was all nerves. He walked restlessly up and down the room that day when I saw him. It was just before the fight in which he lost his championship. Tunney had been in the same place the day before. The photographer, after Dempsey had left, showed me several photographs he had taken of the man Tunney. Beside Dempsey he seemed to me a dilettante, a dilettante with his fists, with his mind, with his feelings.

"He would be self-conscious," I thought. This man is no plunger. He would be a man always thinking, "Now, as I am a prize fighter, I must look fierce." He would be a gentleman. "I must develop my mind."

I could imagine Dempsey going off on almost any sort of angle. He might get drunk, get into a saloon brawl. He might take a sudden and violent fancy for some woman. He might do any generous thing.

Mr. Tunney went off to Europe. He went on a walking trip with a writer. I could fancy them going along the road together. They were both thinking. One was thinking, "Here am I, a man of the mind. I have a close friend who is a prize fighter. How wonderful!" And there was the other thinking, "I am a prize fighter, but I am no brute. I am a man of mind. My being with this writer proves it."

There was a great deal of newspaper talk about all this.

It is true that the man of the mind has always a liking for the man of action. Primitive, simple people appeal to him. He is trying to understand human nature. These self-conscious calculating men do not appeal to him. They are too much like himself.

And he is himself a man of action—in the true sense. The painter, at his easel, when he is really painting, is an excited man. All of his nerves are on edge. I have watched painters at work who were like Dempsey about to enter the prize ring. One man I knew swore violently sometimes when he was painting. If you had interrupted him at such a time he might well have hit you with his fist. He might have beaten you brutally. "Get out of here!"

He was trying to catch some delicate thing. Thoughts and feeling elude like a fast opponent in the ring. You rush at your opponent—the mood. "Oh, if I could only hit it squarely, send it sprawling!"

I remember going once into an apartment in New York. A man I knew lived there, a writer friend. He had invited me to come and dine with him.

I went in the late afternoon. The place was quiet. I went through his workroom. He was in his bedroom, lying on his bed.

He told me later that he had been working for two years trying to get just the feeling he wanted in a certain piece of work. That morning he had got up feeling ill. However, as he sat at breakfast, what he wanted came clear at last. He had written some twelve thousand words during the day. The twelve thousand words were the very heart of a long book. After he wrote them that day he never changed a word. It was marvelous writing.

And what a physical task! All day he had been hitting and hitting. There was perfect timing of the sentences. They rang like bells. I have read over what the man wrote that day a hundred times. I can see no flaw in it.

He told me that on the particular day of which I am now speaking he was so exhausted that by noon he could hardly sit in his chair. He sent out and got a quart of whiskey. During the afternoon he drank it all. "I was drunk later—when I had finished the thing," he told me. "While I worked I was not drunk."

It was a physical test. When I saw him he was so exhausted he could scarcely raise his head from the bed. He was as a prize fighter might have been after a marvelous fight.

As for the Tunney, he was always a bit too patronizing about his trade. He profited by the prize-fighting thing and yet spoke of it with contempt. The being intellectual was a bit too obvious. On my life, Mr. Jack Dempsey, or before him the Negro Jack Johnson, had each of them a better mind.

There is too much of this bunk about a man having a mind because he has read the classics. It was not Mr. Will Shakespeare's fault that Mr. Tunney, after he had retired from the ring with his million, began delivering lectures about Mr. Will Shakespeare's plays.

MR. J. J. LANKES AND
HIS WOODCUTS

MR. J. J. LANKES, the Virginia woodcut man, is really a gentle, quiet man. He goes about looking for little slices of something significant and lovely in commonplace things. Things please him. He has that rare, that charming faculty, so seldom found nowadays, of getting delight out of many little commonplace phases of our everyday life. You frame one of his little woodcuts and put it on the wall of your room. It is a group of trees on a windswept hillside, or a winter scene in a barnyard, or a Virginia village street. There it is. Why, you have yourself seen just such scenes a thousand times. They did not catch your attention, even seemed ugly to you, but now, under the touch of this man's hand, see what they have become.

I am writing of Mr. Lankes on a gray October day. Well, I got up this morning and tried to work. I couldn't. There was a certain scene, a chapter of a book I had planned to write. The words would not flow. They were dead, meaningless things under my hand.

I went out into the street and wandered about. Gray skies looked down at me, and suddenly there was something gray and old and tired about the town I was in and about the people of the town. There were ugly people along the street, ugly people were going in and out of stores. I was myself ugly. "It is on such days as this that murders are done," I said to myself.

There are always murders being done. I am myself always killing the flow of life in myself. "It is all really very simple. The object of life is to live." By living I do not mean dwelling in a big house, having servants to wait on me. I do not mean living in a house hung with expensive and luxurious hangings, drinking rare wines, eating rich foods.

Life in your great house can be as ugly as in the most miserable little mountain cabin or in a tenement in a city. There is a queer sort of separation from the life about us that at times attacks us all, and it is this separation from life that dams up the flow. The damming up is pretty universal nowadays.

Life should be fascinating enough. People everywhere are living, after a fashion, even in times like these. We go on, but it is a spiritually tired time. Who can deny it? Why, so far as I am concerned, my mails are filled with it.

Such desperate letters come to me. There is talk of

suicide, even among the young. "There is no light," people say. "Where is the sun?"

People are wanting to draw nearer to each other— understand each other better, but they cannot do it. It may be because we are all trying on the grand scale.

I prefer company as I eat, some one talking to me. I prefer thoughts. I like things in my dining-room that arouse, that awaken thoughts in me.

So I have these Lankes woodcuts. There is a frame house belonging, let us say, to a merchant. There is an old house in Williamsburg, Virginia.

It isn't much of a house, that one, and never was. It is a little box-like structure, thrown hastily up, a long time ago. Well, not so long ago, perhaps twenty years ago, but look at it now. This is not one of our proud old Virginia mansions of Colonial days. Already it is all warped out of shape. There is a little shed at the back, all askew, and a dilapidated Ford stands in the road. A little washing has been hung out. It is wash day in the house.

There is the sky hanging over all of this. The little house rests upon the breast of mother earth. But let us not be sentimental. Mr. Lankes never is. I honor him for his realism.

The man has feeling. He has that odd quality, so infinitely valuable, the feeling for things, for the reflected life in things. Why, at this moment, I have on my desk before me a letter from Mr. Lankes, himself. I have already told him that I am anxious to write of him. "You let me do it," I have said to him. "I want to do it."

I have a notion I have something to say and he is afraid that I will be writing of himself, the man. He is afraid I will try to draw a character sketch of him.

He has been trying to beguile me. He writes me letters making little drawings on the margins. He wants me to write, not of himself, but of wood cutting. When I have been with him he has talked to me of this craft.

He will talk at length of the various kinds of wood. I am sure I do not quote him correctly, now. Wood cutting is not my craft. "Chestnut is a good wood," he says. I do not remember whether he said chestnut, or oak, or hickory.

I do remember that when I have been with him he spoke of the grain in various woods. "In such and such a wood the grain runs so and so. You look at this piece of wood now. The grain makes these certain convolutions. Look at the end of this piece. Or will you look at this?" He has written me letters. There are little drawings of wood carvers' tools along the margins of the letters.

What I think of Mr. Lankes, what I really want to say of him, is that he has got hold of something lost nowadays to most of us. He is a man who has sensed, who senses constantly, delicately, the reflected things in life.

We should begin with little things.

I am here in this small town street. There are dirty papers, blown by a damp wintry wind into gutters. A sick old woman gets out of a Ford and goes up a dirty stairway to a doctor's office. A woman passes with a child. The child is crying and the mother is indifferent. She fairly drags the child along the street.

What I am trying to say is that there are always these little scenes, presenting themselves for our notice, out of the commonplace little incidents of our everyday lives. They are ugly. Surely. But let them be truly presented, so that we feel them as part of ourselves, and something happens.

Beauty happens. That strange intangible quality of looking at life and at things, feeling into life and things, making others feel, is in everything this man, Lankes, the Virginia woodcut man, is doing.

He is, I think, a very significant man. I have said he is a gentle and a quiet man. Now that I come to think of him, I remember that he is not always so quiet.

He is a man who does not talk readily. There he is, a tall dark man clad in workingmen's clothes. He will be going about so.

He comes to see you or you go to see him. Let us say you take a walk. Lankes will go moodily and silently along. You sit down upon a bridge.

Now he begins to talk. He will begin making little woodcuts with words.

He was in a house once. He tells you about that. The talk has nothing to do with anything that has been said. He was merely going along a road, was sketching along a road. It began to rain and there was an unpainted farmhouse nearby. He went to it and an old woman invited him into the house. He will be telling about what happened.

Nothing much happened.

Now he is talking eagerly. Words flow from him. They roll and tumble from him. While he was in that house . . . the house dropped into casually like that . . . he only stayed until a shower passed . . . not much was said . . . but he saw everything. He will give you a description of the inside of the house or of a room in that house, infinitely detailed, for some queer reason absorbingly interesting.

I spoke of having some of his woodcuts framed in my house. They are in the dining-room. What an odd place for these things, some one says.

Not really. I am not a man absorbed in eating, in that kind of fleshly delight. I do not want painted baskets of fruit or game or fish hung in my dining-room. I am not an Elizabethan. I wish I were.

There is an old fence going up a hill through a pasture.

Look at it, in a Lankes woodcut. There is an old fence and an old gate.

Or, let us say, there is a large woodcut of a barnyard. You see a house in the distance, a farmer's house. It is winter. The farmer's wife got from a fruit-tree agent who came down along the road on which her house stands some young fruit trees. She was a poor woman but she sold eggs and butter in town and got the money to buy these young trees.

She got two peach trees, an apricot, two Bartlett pears and some cherry trees.

The trees were put out two years ago, but the farmer's wife had bad luck with them. Last winter rabbits came into the yard and nibbled at the tender young things. Some of them died in the spring. One day a cow destroyed three trees. She only had a dozen. It got down at last to one tree, a young pear tree, and she got her husband to build a little fence about it. He got some old boards and sticks and put up a kind of fence. There it is. It is just thrown together.

You see it there in a Lankes woodcut and as you look you know the whole story of that poor farmer's wife. You know about her hopes, her disappointments. There is her whole story told in these few sticks awkwardly nailed up there. She herself doesn't appear. You never see her. In spite of yourself you look, your heart filled with anxiety. You do so want the last young tree to live, to bear fruit for that woman.

Mr. Lankes gets at you in this way. He is always getting at you. He is a man deeply concerned with life, but it is his way to get at life through things. He feels always the reflected life in things, in barns, sheds back of barns, in little houses in which poor people live. He is always asserting something. "Look," he says. "Look again. Don't you see it?" He is telling you about something. "It is human life," he says. "Life is here in these inanimate things people have touched.

"Because this old fence, this gate, this old house here, this store to which people come to trade, this cart behind the barn, because these things have been touched by human hands, because they have become a part of this strange muddle we call life, they have become sacred things. See the significance, the beauty in them."

If you cannot see, if what Lankes is always telling you, you cannot see, if life escapes you, it isn't the fault of this man. He at least is doing his part. He is reasserting the life and the beauty buried away in things, is always reasserting it in every woodcut he makes.

It is his determination, his assertion and reassertion, as well as the beauty of his work that, it seems to me, make Lankes, the Virginia woodcut man, one of the very significant living artists of our day.

Why, he is content not to be in the grand tone. He is a modest, a humble man. He isn't loud. There he is, always at work. In a time of low spiritual vitality he is constantly at it, asserting and reasserting in his work the beauty and wonder of everyday life.

TWO
IRISHMEN

IN A HOTEL ROOM . . . in an eastern city . . . on a Sunday morning . . . a newspaper on a bed beside me.

Fred O'Brien's picture is in the paper. "Fred O'Brien died suddenly at Sausalito, California." He had built a house out there on a point of land overlooking San Francisco Bay, the Golden Gate. I went there once— stayed there with him two or three days.

Little Fred. He wasn't a big man. He had a tough, wiry, strong little body . . . a shock of silvery gray hair. It had grayed early, prematurely.

He loved wine, grand clothes, lovely women, books, travel. He was one of the most restless men I have ever known. There were a lot of things about Fred's life moralists would shake their heads over.

He was like another man deeply loved who died this year . . . Maurice Long, at Washington. Maurice was a big man, big of body, strong also, with a big head and a shock of iron-gray hair. Maurice came as a boy from

Ireland, lived a vivid adventurous life, made millions, lost it, threw it away.

Made another fortune. Lost it. Made a third.

Fred and Maurice were both Irish. They were both born Catholics, both left that faith, never went back.

They were both good livers.

"Give me life, lots of it." They both went out eagerly to life. The citizen who stays at home, saves his money, buys a little land, goes to church on Sunday—he and his fellows may be the backbone of the state—of society. I don't know.

Such men would never understand these two men, both of whom I have loved and who are now both dead. They never knew each other although I talked and wrote letters to Maurice about Fred, to Fred about Maurice. They would have loved each other. What a story-telling bout there would have been! It would have meant something just to have the joy of sitting on one side and listening.

Two tender, alive, imaginative Irishmen. Whatever gods haunt the hills and vales of Ireland—St. Patrick?— I thank thee that I have known and loved these two men.

Talk . . . tales being told . . . the flow of ideas, images, scenes remembered, strange adventures.

Maurice died as he would have liked to have died—in the early fall, walking in a field by a creek—his horse and dog were with him. It was a little hound dog. I was with him when he bought it. "You may name it," he said.

"All right," I said. "We'll call it Andy Funk," giving the dog the name of a third friend.

So there was Maurice, that glorious Irishman walking across a field, leading his horse. He stopped. Perhaps he looked up at the clouds. He fell down dead. Andy Funk gave a little yipping bark. That was all.

He died as he would have wanted to die, as one of his friends said, "with his pants on."

Big Irishman, little Irishman . . . both dead. They were the two best story-tellers I ever knew.

Never losing the balance of a tale; catching, in talk, the pathos of lives; understanding, tender, imaginative men.

The last time I saw Fred O'Brien was in New Orleans. He had got comfortably well-to-do with a book, "White Shadows in the South Seas." He came to New Orleans to spend a week with me.

It was spring. He went one morning before he left to lie on the docks beside the Mississippi River.

There were ships. There was the brown river in the spring flood.

It started Fred on his own life, a wandering strange life in all the seven seas, islands, brown people, yellow people, back countries. He talked a thousand times better than he ever wrote.

It is good to have known such a man in a lifetime, to have had that kind of day with him.

Scenes remembered, places, people, tenderly, with rich imaginative understanding. "What is a good man? What is goodness? What is the good life?"

Maurice died in the fall. For days after the time of his death my room was haunted by his presence. At night I dreamed. Other men and women I knew and loved kept coming to me in my dreams. They dragged Maurice, the big Irishman, into my room, holding his hand. "See, he isn't dead," they said, and now today, all day, my room will be haunted by another one, by the little Irish story-teller, Fred O'Brien . . . who died suddenly in his house at Sausalito . . . the house with the windows looking out to the Pacific . . . through the Golden Gate.

TO
GEORGE BORROW

I THINK THAT EVERY writer who loves writing for its own sake—word lovers who have a feeling for word against word—the color, sound, smell of words on a page (how many even among famous writers there are who do not have the feeling)— all such must have some other and older writer who is to him the great master.

I remember how and when I found mine.

George Borrow—to me the great writer.

I was in Ohio, a young man. I had got into business, was a manufacturer. I had a wife and family.

The yen for writing had, however, taken hold of me. There was a man of the town to which I had come who was the editor of the local daily. Occasionally he came to me. "Here is a situation. Write an editorial for me."

There was a socialist leader of the town who wrote an open letter to the editor, attacking its policy. "I dare you to print it."

The editor did and then came running to me. "You must answer it for me."

I did and there was a knock on my door. It was the socialist leader. "I want your help. Here is this article in the paper. Sit down here and write an answer to it."

That also I did. The controversy between my right and my left hand was carried on for two or three weeks. It was fierce. At last I got the two men into a bar-room and told them what I had been doing. Revolutionists should never trust scribblers. The scribblers have their own fish to fry.

The three of us got drunk together. I am not sure that the drinking healed the wounds I had made.

There was a woman came to that town. Blessings be upon her head. Is she still alive? She was dark and slender, a school teacher. Do not worry, dear reader. This is not to be a story of a man and woman in love.

I had begun wandering in the woods about the town and the woman, mentioned above, was also fond of long solitary walks.

But this also should be explained. At the time of which I speak I was deeply dissatisfied with my life. I was making money. Is there any way of making money without feeling as I then felt? I have not found it.

I was continually lying and cheating. No one seemed to care. I was prospering. Why did I so mind such lying?

There are other kinds of lying I have never minded at all.

I was unhappy. I got drunk. I was bored. I did not know what was the matter with me. It was at that time I began writing novels and stories. I fixed up a room in my house, had a desk and plenty of ink and paper. I kept the door locked and the key in my pocket. To my wife and the servant I said harshly, "Keep out of that room. If it needs cleaning I will clean it myself."

"I am working some things out in there," I said, trying to be mysterious.

I was trying to work something out but now I know that, from the viewpoint of the writer, everything I did in the room was corrupt. I had said to myself, "I cannot understand myself and my own motives in life. Very well, to hell with self. I will invent imaginary figures, throw them into life. Some of them will be having just such experiences of American life as I am having."

What I did was corrupt because I was doing it to save myself. I did not like the idea of being what I thought I was becoming. It is obvious to me now that I was trying to find a patent medicine, a kind of cure-all for my own good.

Oh, my soul—to the flames with you too!

So one day I was walking in a wood by a river near the town and there was the little dark slender woman, the school teacher, who had also gone for a solitary walk, and she was sitting under a tree by a stream and reading a book.

But let me not be trying to make a mystery of this matter. I had already met the woman. At that time I had social ambitions. I was making money, had still the reputation of being a bright young business man. Occasionally, in the evening, I put on evening clothes and sallied forth.

It may be that I wanted a lot of women to fall in love with me, that I thought, "If they do, it will set me up—give me more confidence in myself."

At any rate, there was the woman sitting under the tree by the stream and reading the book. I approached along a path. She did not hear me coming. I stopped and stood looking at her.

At first, no doubt, as I stood as described, looking at the woman, I did look at her as such men as I was at that time do look at women. It may be that I was absorbed, looking at the enticing figure, the straight legs, the good ankles, the slender feet.

I am very sure that she had a slender neck and that the head was delicately posed.

But bosh! This is not what I am trying to say. I stood at gaze and as I stood my eyes became fixed upon the book held in her hands. She was absorbed in its pages.

She was a Borrovian, the first one I had ever seen. At that time I had not even heard the name of Borrow.

Oh, sweet master of the trivial, of the everyday little adventures of living, hater of sham respectability! Oh, great man, thou absurd fellow, great prose master, George Borrow!

I have always held firmly to the opinion that from certain books—if you be yourself a book lover—if you are not trying to improve your mind through books but have yourself a pure enough soul so that you may read for the pure pleasure of reading—as you would swim in the sea, or drink a glass of rare wine, or love a beautiful woman . . . having this purity of soul I maintain that it is entirely possible for something to happen to you in relation to the works of certain other writers—it happened to Borrow himself. Readers of Borrow will remember the incident when Borrow was a youth.

His mind was clouded. He was puzzled and unhappy. Listen to him. He is ill, of the dread of life we have all known and is lying on a couch.

.   .   .   .

"What ails you, my child?" said the mother to her son, as he lay on a couch under the influence of the dreadful one: "what ails you? You seem afraid."

Boy. "And so I am: a dreadful fear is upon me."

Mother. "But of what: there is no one can harm you; of what are you apprehensive?"

Boy. "Of nothing that I can express: I know not what I am afraid of, but afraid I am."

Mother. "Perhaps you see sights and visions: I knew a lady once who was continually thinking that she saw an armed man threaten her, but it was only an imagination, a phantom of the brain."

Boy. "No armed man threatens me; and 'tis not a thing like that would cause me any fear. Did an armed man threaten me I would get up and fight him; weak as I am, I would wish for nothing better, for then, perhaps, I should lose this fear; mine is a dread of I know not what, and there the horror lies."

Mother. "Your forehead is cool and your speech collected. Do you know where you are?"

Boy. "I know where I am, and I see things just as they are; you are beside me, and upon the table there is a book which was written by a Florentine; all of this I see and that there is no ground for being afraid. I am, moreover, quite cool, and feel no pain—but, but ——"

And then there was a burst of "gemiti, sospiri ed alti guai. Alas, alas, poor child of clay as the sparks fly upward, so wast thou born to sorrow."

There is an incident in Borrow. It is in *Lavengro*,
pages 16 and 17 in my copy, published in 1851 by John
Murray, Albemarle Street, London. A young lady had
come to the house of Borrow's mother and had brought
a package of books. There was one for young George—
Defoe's Robinson Crusoe. But let Borrow himself tell of
what happened.

"I remember for some time sitting motionless in
my corner, with my eyes bent upon the ground; at
last I lifted my head and looked upon the packet
as it lay upon the table. All at once a strange sensa-
tion came over me, such as I had never experienced
before—a singular blending of curiosity, awe and
pleasure, the remembrance of which, even at this
distance of time, produces a remarkable effect upon
my nervous system. What strange things are the
nerves—I mean those more secret and mysterious
ones in which I have some notion that the mind or
soul, call it which you will, has its habitation, how
they occasionally tingle and vibrate before any
coming event closely connected with the future weal
or woe of the human being. Such a feeling was now
within me, certainly independent of what the eye
had seen or the ear had heard. A book of some
description had been brought for me, a present by
no means calculated to interest me; what cared I

for books? I had already many into which I had
never looked but from compulsion, friends, moreover, had presented me with similar things before,
which I had entirely disregarded, and what was there
in this particular book, whose very title I did not
know, calculated to attract me more than the rest?
Yet something within told me that my fate was
connected with the book that had been last brought;
so, that after looking at the packet from my corner
for a considerable time, I got up and went to the
table."

.   .   .   .

As it was with Borrow and Defoe, so it was with me
and Borrow. But two other writers have affected me so—
Turgenev and Moore.

And so I approached the woman, the school teacher,
by the stream. If she be still alive, may she have had
a blessed life. I stood beside her and my hands trembled.

"I have a great curiosity. Something has happened
to me.

"That book you have in your hand."

She was the first Borrovian I had ever known.

"It is a great book," she said.

"I do not know why it is," she added, "but I hesitate
about introducing any one to this Borrow.

"There is a fear," she explained. "It is quite possible you may find the book very dull."

"But no," I cried, "give it to me."

"You mean?" she asked. Oh, what beautiful eyes she had! They were gray eyes and now looked steadily at me.

"You mean that you have already, never having touched one of his books, that already you have felt the charm?"

"But it is coming to me through the very covers of the book, held there in your hand," I cried.

"It is as the charm that sometimes emanates from a woman ——

"I am sorry if I have seemed to place a limit upon your own charm ——

"It is very strong but that of the book is at the moment much stronger."

.   .   .   .

It was thus that I was introduced to that great master of prose, Mr. George Borrow. The woman by the stream must have been very wise. None but Borrovians will believe this tale.

And what extraordinary people they are—the Borrovians. Oh, little band of the faithful, I salute thee!

The woman by the stream was one of us. She gave me the book—Mr. Borrow's "Bible in Spain"—she that day held in her hand, and afterward, during many afternoons—I dare say there was scandal enough talked about us in the Ohio town—we walked often enough, through the streets of the town and out into the fields.

It was one of the real friendships of my life.

"And do you think . . ."

"Listen to this ——"

There was for me a discovery. Often enough since have I wandered from the true path.

I have wanted to change people, reform them, convince them.

"Do not do it!" I have cried to myself.

"Write! Write! It is enough."

But who am I to tell how that should be done? Let me turn to the great one, the prose master. I stop writing and go to my bookcase. There is my own Borrow complete, bound in beautiful leather. I take down a volume and open at random.

Why, here is Borrow describing his experience in a law office. He has set out to describe the man with whom he is reading law. Let me read it to you:

> "I wish I could describe him, for I loved the man, and with reason, for he was ever kind to me, to whom kindness has not always been shown; and he was, moreover, a choice specimen of a class which no longer exists—a gentleman lawyer of the old school. I would fain describe him, but figures with

whom he had nought to do press forward and keep
him from my mind's eye; there they pass, Spaniard
and Moor, Gypsy, Turk and livid Jew. But who is
that? What that pursy man in the loose, snuff-
colored great-coat, with the white stockings, drab
breeches, and silver buckles on his shoes? That man
with the bull neck and singular head, immense in
the lower part, especially about the jaws, but taper-
ing upward like a pear; the man with the busy
brows, small grey eyes, replete with cat-like expres-
sion, whose grizzled hair is cut close, and whose ear-
lobes are pierced with small golden rings?"

Aha! And so Mr. George ——

But what has he you describe so vividly to do with
the man you set out to describe?

"Why, nothing at all."

"And so—you are a writer—and what a glorious one."

"I was about to tell you many details in the life of a
certain respectable old gentleman and then this other—
you see he popped into my head."

And so.

And so, dear George, you thought of nothing but
writing?

"You were the pure one. You had faith even in your
own prejudices, your own hatreds. You went on a writing
jag—didn't you, George?

"Having taken your pen in hand and having set yourself down to write you cared for nothing but the beauty and glory of writing.

"It is that, dear George, that has made you what you are to us—your followers. We are a small band but we shall ever be faithful to you.

"We are yours, dear George, we, the Borrovians.

"For your purity, dear George, is a very special purity. It is something that many of the so-called great among writers will never understand.

"For it has in it always, on every page, always present, the curious purity, the true morality that is the only true purity and morality for all of us who follow your trade."

A STONEWALL JACKSON MAN

O<small>N</small> AUGUST TENTH of this year (1934) there died, at the home of John Woods of Grayson County, Virginia, a fine old commoner, George W. Sells. He was almost ninety-three years old and except for a short interval, had lived all of his life in the one mountain community. The interval was full of rich meaning for him.

Mr. Sells left Grayson County, Virginia, when he was a young man to go into the Confederate army and to become a Stonewall Jackson man and he was with Jackson in the swift marches, the plunging attacks and the determined stands that made Jackson what Lee called "his right arm."

They didn't begin to get Lee until Jackson was gone, shot by accident by one of his own men in the same battle . . . the bloody battle of Chancellorsville . . . in which battle the mountain man George Sells was also desperately wounded.

The bullet that got George went through his upper

47

arm as he was raising the arm to fire. The ball went on into his shoulder making a great hole, and lodged there, stayed there until he died.

In the last five years of his life the old man, a thin tough-fibered old fellow, rode often past my Virginia house. We stopped many times to talk by a bridge or under a tree beside the road and we talked always of the Civil War.

"And did you go by the Furnace Road and then by the Brock Road to get to Hooker's flank?"

"Yes. In the night."

In every battle there must be a moment. Grant knew and Lee knew. "Wait until they think you are licked and then turn upon them." Grant at Shiloh and Lee at Chancellorsville. Joe Hooker, the Northern general, sending messages to Washington. "Lee is licked," *etc.* It is exciting to talk to a man who has taken part in such a moment.

It was a turning point in the war, when Lee began to thrust desperately into the North, the thrust that ended at Gettysburg, and in Washington Lincoln was desperate. He had tried McClellan and then Burnside, who got his at Fredericksburg.

And then came Joe Hooker, called "Fighting Joe." Joe was a good deal the braggart. He talked too much and too big. He had even gone about talking of a dictatorship . . . "What this country needs is a dictator."

Nevertheless Lincoln put him in there to stop Lee and at Chancellorsville Hooker thought he had done it. "You give us victories and I'll take care of the dictatorships," Lincoln had said to Hooker.

And Hooker thought he had done it until Stonewall Jackson made his march.

Another quick march, in the late day, in the night, by little country roads . . . George Sells, the Grayson County Virginia boy, marching with the others at the heels of Stonewall Jackson's horse. O thou grim Presbyterian!

Through the woods, past little old Virginia houses, much like Southern mountaineers' houses. "There goes Stonewall Jackson and his men. Look out, Hooker."

There was Howard, trying to feel his way around Lee's flank when Jackson and his men came roaring down at them.

(Me, to George Sells, on a country road.)

"And did you give 'em the Rebel yell?"

"We did that."

"And would you give me a sample of it now? I'm a Yank, you know."

He did. He sat on his horse and I was standing beside the horse in a country road. He stood up in his stirrups and there was a wild yell, half scream. The cry itself seemed like a living thing, flying over the hills, under the trees, and I shivered, hearing it. It may have

been some old Yank tribal fear in me, hearing the yell
on a rainy day in the Virginia hills.

So there was George Sells coming down, "out of the
wilderness," with the Stonewall Jackson men, they giving
that yell, Howard's forces crumbling up before the attack, another Northern disaster . . . "goodbye, fighting
Joe Hooker, thou windy one . . . make way for Meade
now and presently for Grant . . . another Westerner,
like Hooker, but no braggart.

"Old Joe Hooker.
Won't you come out of the wilderness.
Out of the wilderness,
Out of the wilderness."

Jackson's men roaring down on Howard and, at the
same moment, Lee was himself on the move.

They got George Sells. He went down, lay writhing on
the ground, blood spurting from his wounds.

"How long did you lie there?"

He said it must have been many hours. They didn't
get to him, to cart him in to the field hospital, until the
next day. They dropped him there. He said doctors kept
going past him. "Look here," he cried, "I want some
attention here."

Now and then a doctor would stop for a moment, look
down at him, take a look at his wounds. "I'd take your

arm off, man, but it's no use. You'll be dead in an hour. There are men here who have a chance for life."

"Dead, eh?"

George Sells chuckled telling me of it. The doctors were like Joe Hooker. They were too cock-sure. "I told 'em: 'I'll live past all of ye,' and I have. They told me that and they're all dead now and I'm here and I've got my arm.

"I got my Yankee bullet too. It's flat there, against the bone of my shoulder." The old man chuckled the last time he told me about it. He gave me, at my request, the Rebel yell again.

Mr. George Sells was a sturdy American commoner, a farmer. He worked hard all of his life on the land. He acquired land, a strip of woods here, a valley bottom piece there. He asked favors of no man. He was a man worth knowing. He was a good neighbor. He died, at ninety-three, August tenth, nineteen hundred and thirty-four at the home of John Woods, in Grayson County, Virginia.

LINCOLN STEFFENS TALKS
OF RUSSIA

When I was recently in the far west, on the Pacific coast, I went for the day to the house of Mr. Lincoln Steffens.

Mr. Steffens has been, during a rather exciting lifetime, the friend and intimate of many prominent men—of Theodore Roosevelt, Woodrow Wilson, Clarence Darrow, Lenin and Stalin in Russia, and of many others. For the last ten years now he has been interested in the Russian experiment in government and has been in Russia many times. He was there during the first revolution, when Kerensky came into power and then later during the Bolshevik Revolution.

I went at his invitation to spend a day at his house. It was a lovely place in the town of Carmel-by-the-Sea, near the Pacific. The roar of breaking waves could almost be heard from his garden and I dare say during storms it could be clearly heard. The garden itself was a sea of flowers. Because of the temperate climate out there flowers grow in mad profusion. Mr. Steffens had recently completed the two-volume story of his own life which had a big sale. He was for a long time looked upon as America's star reporter. Theodore Roosevelt had once called him the best reporter in America.

He is a rather small man with a soft voice and is very successful as a public speaker. I have noticed that most of our orators—lawyers addressing jurors in our Court House, political speakers and others—when, in making a public address, they want to emphasize a point, they begin to shout. Once I heard a lawyer in a Court House in a Southern town shouting so loudly that I thought he must at least be pleading for some prisoner's life. So I hurried to the Court House. He was trying to collect damages for a cow hit by an automobile.

In a public address men like Clarence Darrow and Lincoln Steffens always speak rather softly. When they want to strengthen a point, emphasize a point, they are inclined to lower their voices and make them even softer. Often the voice is dropped almost to a whisper. It is peculiarly effective. The man seems to say to you, "Well, here is a point I do not need to emphasize. It is so obviously true." You find yourself taken unaware. You believe what the speaker is saying.

I walked about and sat with Mr. Lincoln Steffens in the garden back of his house while he talked with me at length of his experiences in Russia.

In Russia there are comparatively few of the kind of middle-class people who, upon the whole, dominate American life. At the top when Steffens first knew the country, there was the aristocracy, and below, a vast nation of peasants. Industry had just begun to come to Russia and in the cities there was a growing class of industrial workers.

The old Russian government was very corrupt, to tell the truth, just about as corrupt as some sections of our own government. When the great war came hundreds of thousands of soldiers, coming of course out of the peasant and working classes . . . it is almost always the poor who in a war go to the front and get killed . . . were sent into the trenches, often with terribly poor equipment. The Russian manufacturers of ammunition scamped their jobs and the Allies sent into the country inferior equipment for which they charged the Russians tremendous prices. Debts grew and taxes were heavy while at the front the Russians, with their inferior war materials, were killed like flies by the better equipped Germans. Naturally, the soldiers became disheartened and finally refused to fight any more. They had had enough of being killed for nothing. The revolutionary impulse ran through the whole working population. There came a cry of anguish from the peasants whose sons were being mercilessly slaughtered. The first revolution came.

There was an effort to establish a democratic government much like our own, but the Allies at once insisted that the troops go back into the trenches. Every effort was made to pump up enthusiasm. All the Allies sent men to Russia to urge the people to keep on fighting. They did not do it. They refused.

Kerensky, with the few troops he could command, tried to force the soldiers back into the trenches and into battle. The guns of Russians were turned against Russians.

At that moment Lenin appeared. He and his Bolshevik followers had a definite program. He said, "We will take the land away from the aristocracy. We will take the factories away from the owners. All the products of the Russian fields and the Russian factories shall go to the Russian people."

All of this Mr. Lincoln Steffens had seen from the beginning. He had known personally all the leaders of the movement in Russia and had had many talks with them. He believed in their sincerity and he believes that the experiment will work. It was absorbing to walk about a garden among the flowers, with this sensitive and expert observer, and to hear from his lips the story of what is going on in Russia. You got, at any rate, from this man, a sense of a people who in this confused time feel they are building. They are not living in the past, but in the future. Belief has come to them. If thousands of other Americans could have had the experience I had, listening to the gentle Steffens talk in his garden, the belief in what the Russians are trying to do would spread like a flame.

NO
SWANK

IN THE MOUNTAIN
country of southwest Virginia, Kentucky and Tennessee,
they say of a man, meaning to pay him the highest possible compliment, "Oh, he's just common," they say.
They mean he isn't high hat, that he doesn't think that
God has made him nobler, braver or wiser than other
men, that he doesn't look down at you from some great
height, you know, being nice to you and kindly and all
that but . . .

. . . but but but but but . . .

And what a lot of but but butting there is in this
world! I think it must come from fear. A lot of things
come from fear. A man is secretly afraid he isn't first
class. So he begins to assert first-classness. He gets like
the woman who talks too much of her purity.

But I sat down here today to speak of a certain man,
Mr. Henry Wallace, now Secretary of Agriculture in the
Cabinet of President Roosevelt. I have fondness for this
man, admiration for him. He was born at such and such

a place. His eyes are of such and such a color. Well, you know, little illuminating anecdotes told. Really I should know how a piece like this, about a public man, should be written. I have read enough of them. You get some pictures for your piece. Henry as a child. Then as a high-school boy. Perhaps he once did a heroic deed, saved another boy from drowning, or ran a Ford car down a river bank to save a little girl who was walking in the road. You know that one about Abe Lincoln, how he was clerking as a young man in a country store and made a mistake, of say five cents, in the change given a country woman who had bought some tea and how he at once closed the store and walked ten miles . . . there must have been a blizzard blowing . . . through the dense forests, *etc., etc.,* to give it back to her.

Now I will bet that Henry Wallace never did anything like that and if he ever did and I knew it and told it I'll bet he'd cut my acquaintance . . . and he should, too.

I think the fair thing, if I can do it, is to give rather an impression, but to do that I'll have to approach rather by the back door.

Two years ago this winter I was in the South. I went down there because, first of all, I like being in the South and then besides, just at that time, I was intensely interested in factories. So I went down and spent the winter, mostly in factories, and I got to know a lot of factory workers.

You can guess what they were. They were "poor whites."

I went around with them a good deal, sitting with them in their houses in the mill villages and going with them, whenever they'd let me, into the factories. I couldn't get into a lot of factories. They had heard I was a radical. So I associated a lot with the factory workers, ate supper with them, walked around and smoked cigarettes with them, talked things over with them. I was told that about half of them couldn't read or write, but I didn't ask. I didn't want to embarrass any one.

One night I went off with a lot of these people to a dance. If I remember rightly this was at Columbus, Georgia. There was a little hall, rather crowded, and it was hot.

I sat there, rather on the side lines.

With me, sometimes . . . well, I get into a certain state. It happened that night. There might have been three hundred people, men and women, boys and girls, in the hall. There were these unfortunate people. Poor, poor things! They didn't have any swell clothes. It was hot that night and all the men were dancing in their shirt sleeves. Why, I do not want to minimize the position they were in. Most of them worked like driven dogs.

There was a sense of heavy weariness in the hot little hall.

It may have affected me. I got into a kind of half coma, sitting aside and watching.

And then this thing happened. I began to pick out figures, men and women, from among these dancing mill hands, these poor whites.

There are certain people who strike upon your consciousness in a certain way and it happens that I am a man of rather large acquaintance. It has been my luck to know, often quite intimately, Americans of almost every possible sort, rich successful Americans, poor destitute American bums, thieves, prize fighters, a few society men and women, country storekeepers, figures in the world of art and of science. I won't go on. You get my notion. The point is that being in that little hall and watching the dancing mill hands I began that night to pick out from among them as they danced past me figures of men and women I had known in other worlds. I remember that I picked out the Virginia Senator, Carter Glass, the New York critic, Harry Hanson, George Jean Nathan, Jane Addams, the historian Ferdinand Schevill, Benny Leonard the prize fighter, a boy I once saw in jail at Richmond, Virginia, an Ohio small town grocer who was my boyhood friend . . .

I think it is a thing we all do but in it there is something implied that is pretty often forgotten. After all,

America is as yet, and in spite of our bankers, our big industrialists and the other, so-called American kings, a democracy. It really is. Don't think it isn't. I believe that too many of us who write books and articles like this, we intellectuals, highbrow and lowbrow, Washington correspondents for newspapers . . . you will see how it is, nowadays we are all again suddenly interested in government . . . for a long long time, now, government in America has been rather a joke . . . it's the truth . . . a play like "Of Thee I sing" running for a solid year in New York . . . the same sort of thing going on wherever men gather at the backs of country stores in towns, at farmers' gatherings . . . "how can a decent man go into politics in this country?" . . . you know that sort of thing.

So that it gets to be a proof of intellectual integrity that you do not take anything seriously. And there is something all wrong with that, too, for how can you have any fun in life if you are not serious?

I dare say that any one who has read with me thus far will be saying, "But wait. I thought you were going to talk to us about a man, an individual, one Henry Wallace."

But I am talking about him. That's the point. I am trying to talk about him by setting forth how being with this man, talking to him, feeling him—I think, in my own way—how all of this affected me, the thoughts the experience stirred up in me.

You see it is like this . . . there is a great stir in America just now. This great big glorious individualistic thing we had built up here, every man having the right to trample every other man, survival of the fittest . . . no one ever stopping to ask the simple question, "fittest for what?" . . . the thing has apparently cracked. It wobbles on its base and its base is the individual.

. . . his rights, his rights, his rights . . .

"I won't let any one tell me how to run my farm, my newspaper, my factory, my store."

And underneath all of this there is, I think, in America just now, perhaps more than anywhere else in the world, a curious uncertainty, a constant assertion of something that none of us really, deep down in us, believes in. You have to be an American to understand the Americans. I swear you do. There is here a curious earth sense, an odd sense of fellowship-individual brutality so often mixed with an almost unbelievable humility.

For example, this notion, abroad over the world, that Americans are materialists, that they are a money-minded people. Was there ever a notion more absurd? Money-minded people do not blow in their money. They keep it, hide it away, guard it. Look how the Americans blow it in. The successful rich American has gone after it, to be sure, grabbed, lied and cheated often enough to get it, but, if you dig down into him, you will find that, although he may have got possessions, possessions are only in a very secondary way what he is after. He is after something much more gaudy than that.

And wouldn't it be funny if we were to find out that what he is after is a curious thing called civilization?

To be civilized men and women, have a sense of civilization, of something a little dim yet perhaps in the future . . . the whole thing rather perverted just now— grant that.

There is this desire among men, here in America just now, to like and understand each other. It is a pretty dominant hunger among us. I can't help feeling that this thing we are going through, this depression, men and women hungry, suffering, out of work, the spiritual stress and strain of all this . . . the old prosperous, proud, cock-sure America in some queer way blown up, rows of staring blank-eyed factories in industrial towns, Wall Street men who were but yesterday millionaires now broke and knowing the common man's fear of the future . . . there is or should be at least some chance for something humanizing to grow out of all this, and it is needed, for the successful Americans of the past have been about the most lonely people in the world. Individualism and loneliness always go together.

So there is need of finding each other and as Americans finding men we can like.

And that brings me squarely up to Henry Wallace. The man comes from a pretty solid line of Middle-western Americans, land men, a little more than semi-public men for a long time now . . . his father, also named Henry, was Secretary of Agriculture, through both the Harding and Coolidge administrations . . . he had a lot easier ride than this one is going to have . . . already, since this particular smiling, half shy, half Abraham Lincoln-looking Henry has been in the saddle, there has been more kicking, rearing, bucking, dog-falling, *etc., etc.,* than his Pa could ever have known in all of his eight, ten or was it twelve years at it . . .

. . . ride 'em, cowboy . . .

Boy, he'll have to ride.

I said to him . . . this wasn't in Washington, in his office, but in another place. This was on a morning in an orchard. He had been at it six months then and I thought he looked tired.

I was curious. These public men have always aroused my curiosity but this one didn't look to me like a public man . . . you know, one of these fellows who so scare you with a certain side they put on . . . he seemed to me what am I trying to talk about here . . . I mean a man who might just as well have been postmaster in an Ohio town, or a good race-horse driver, or say an auctioneer . . . I don't dare say a first-rate bar-tender, I don't want to hurt Henry . . . he might run for an elective office some day . . .

So I was looking at him and thinking . . . as any one would think, being with him, liking him as I've said, thinking . . . "He's a pretty swell guy but he looks to me too sensitive for the game he's in" . . . thinking as I said it . . . "Lord, I am pretty strong myself, but I couldn't stand that racket . . ."

You see this Henry Wallace doesn't strike you as a fighter. There isn't any of the Teddy Roosevelt in him.

. . . thinking about the "gimme" men who must cluster around him . . .

. . . sugar men . . .

. . . corn men . . .

. . . hog men . . .

Oh, Washington, thou fair capital city!

. . . damn crazy town, too . . .

. . . thinking, as I walked with him and looked at him, of the swell chance he had to stay in Iowa and be editor of *Wallace's Farmer*, a nice, quiet, you know, agricultural paper . . .

. . . letters coming in from the home folks . . . "I had seventeen hogs and we got some slop from a restaurant in town and fed it to them and they all died" . . . "The cow is sick and she is the only cow we've got. We can't renew our subscription. The neighbors say she's got a disease they call hollow tail, but our county agent, he says there isn't any such disease. Is there? . . ."

. . . chance to stay in Iowa and get life nice and homely like that or to go out into the cornfields, or into the hog lot. You see I know that country myself . . .

. . . the long cornfields . . .

. . . the young corn sticking up out of the black ground in the early spring, so shrill green and nice . . .

. . . the tall fat strong upstanding Iowa, Illinois, Indiana and Iowa corn in August . . .

. . . cornfields in the late fall. Farmer boys with chapped hands breaking the big golden ears out of their husks in October.

. . . quiet talk out there in the fields, between men, men's talk . . .

You get my point, fragrance of all this on a man, on this Henry Wallace man and what happens when such a man gets away from all this, his experiments in corn and hog breeding, going to farmers' meetings, editing his *Wallace's Farmer*, playing about in the evening with his boy, Bob . . .

. . . hot long evenings in Middlewestern towns . . .

. . . neighbors met and talked to . . .

. . . something slow, quiet and nice . . .

. . . you throw this against life now in Washington, New York, Cleveland, Detroit, Minneapolis . . .

. . . owners of big lines of grain elevators . . .

. . . sugar magnates . . . Smoot of Utah . . . (oh, I forgot. He is not there any more) . . . bankers, milk dealers, butter dealers . . . fellows with nice suits of clothes on . . . smooth guys . . . rotten guys . . . angry guys . . .

"Christ was born on Christmas day." The phrase ran through my mind as I talked with Henry, that morning when we walked in an orchard, I thought he looked more than reasonably tired. What I said was, "How the hell do you stand it?"

"What?" he said.

"All these guys," I said.

He looked puzzled. The man has got a social sense I haven't got and never will get. I swear if some one were to appoint me to some big official position and I had to take the job and couldn't get out of it, I'd get a gun and blow my brains out and get on home. So I was like a child asking some grown-ups a question when I asked him that . . .

. . . "if I were you and all of these guys . . . gimme, gimme, gimme . . .

. . . "you know, man . . . hungry individualists who have got caught up with during this depression . . . this sudden looking to government to save us . . . government thus getting into a new relationship with our daily lives . . . most of us being still individualists enough to want, first of all, individual salvation . . ."

I was thinking of all this, walking that morning with the man, Henry Wallace of Iowa, in an orchard. He had stopped for a few hours with me, en route, rushing from one point in the country to another . . . a four-hundred-mile drive on the day before . . . three hundred to be covered that day . . .

What a comparatively cool, quiet life my own . . . making my living by pounding out pieces like this.

Conference with . . .

. . . sugar men . . .

. . . hog men . . .

. . . cattle men . . .

. . . cotton men . . .

. . . tobacco men . . .

This agrarian thing in America becomes suddenly terrifically big and important. Sporadic farmers' rebellions breaking out in the West and Southwest.

"He'll get more than one good cursing out."

There would be cause enough for the outbreaks among desperate farmers and no man would know it better than this Henry Wallace, with his farm experience, intimates among the experts in agricultural colleges, experience in running a Middlewestern farm paper.

A sudden centering of all of this upon himself.

In the long and so often greedy building up of industrial America the farmer so much left out. Long lean years of hard and often brutal labor with little enough economic reward, even before the breakdown.

Then something like Hope, a new promise. That would be pretty dangerous, too.

It would inevitably be a good deal like a fire breaking out in a huge building filled with people, the building having but one small and narrow exit.

Now they all rush for the exit. Look! See men, women and children being trampled. See the jam of people there in the dark by the wall. They will be hurting, even killing each other . . . the one hope being that all in the building be quiet and orderly now. Let them be determined but orderly. We are not strong enough as yet to push the walls of the building out.

Now and then, on such occasions . . . I have myself seen it happen two or three times, at fires and strike riots, a man or woman standing out a little from among us. It is a fine thing about America. Such men and women do appear and the leader on such an occasion is rarely the obvious leader sort. There will be some quiet fellow, some fellow we all instinctively know and trust. He gets up smiling. Doesn't talk too loudly. He is the kind of man I am trying to speak about here, making out of all this word slinging a kind of picture of a particular man . . .

. . . who might, as I have said before, as well have been today, farmer, college professor in some small

Middlewestern college, country town storekeeper, country town postmaster. I think Will Rogers is the type, he just accidentally being a big movie star. There is something in common between Will Rogers and Henry Wallace. There is the same little smile . . . an inner rather than an outward smile . . . perhaps just at bottom, a sense of the place in life of the civilized man . . . no swank . . . something that gives us confidence.

"I may not solve anything for you, probably won't, but I won't let you down, sell you out. I won't lie to you. I won't tell you one thing when I mean another."

I asked him the question that morning in the orchard . . . "Say, Mister Sir, how do you stand it? What do you want to do it for?" I wanted to hear what he'd say, but he took his time answering. It may be he didn't know why.

And then suddenly I knew what he would say.

"I guess I didn't put myself into this. I guess I'm in. I'll ride along." He meant, I think, that if you do not think you are the great poobah you do not have to worry much whether you turn out to be one or not.

All of this giving me a sharp sense of something I like and that I think most Americans still instinctively like. It's civilization, isn't it?

. . . a sense of something a little fluid, movement, government itself in flux . . .

on back streets in country towns on summer evenings, men who like each other and like to talk together.

The man was given a desk of his own in another office. I presume he also had his bells to punch, his secretaries and underling.

But he had to jump for Henry's bell.

He said he did. He was telling me about the first time he ever did it. The bell jangled, he said, and he lit out for Henry's office. He said he had been listening to the others and so when he went in he called Henry "Mister Secretary."

He said that Henry stood that all right and told him, in his quiet way, what he wanted and that he started for the door. This, it seems was on an evening in the summer. I was thinking, he said, as I made for the door, of other evenings when I had been with Henry . . .

"You know," he said, "we've been together to shows of fat cattle and corn growing contests, *etc.*

"We'd had our talks together all right, so I took a look back at him and he was standing by his desk and looking down at it and he was smiling at something and at the same time I saw tears on his cheeks."

.   .   .   .

It does look as though Russia would succeed at something. Apparently men in government in Russia are succeeding in an effort to lift a primitive agricultural people across at least a century and to set them down in the midst of industrialism. They may do it, but that isn't our problem. Our problem is apparently to lift a whole race of so-called individualists out of individualism and into civilization. It will take very sincere and human and civilized men of the Henry Wallace sort to do that.

VISIT
TO A PAINTER

I AM IN THE HOUSE OF a painter in a suburb twenty miles from New York. It is an old house on a side street of an old town. The sun is shining outside. Through a window I can see the warm yellow sunlight on an old stone wall. I hear the man's wife moving about the house. He is a man past fifty who has got him a young wife.

The man is in his studio nearby tacking canvas on a frame for a new painting. A half hour ago he was talking to me of what he hopes to do with his canvas. I had been down to the main street of the town and had brought him back a bunch of yellow flowers and he wants to paint them. Already he has made a sketch.

The flowers will stand in a vase, the light streaming in on them from a window.

It is one thing to conceive of such a painting and another to realize it. The painter knows that, and I know. The drawing he had already made is nothing.

"Everything is in color," he said, going out of the

room where he has left me sitting in order that I may write of my adventures here in this world of artists.

He has, however, left some paintings for me to look at as I write.

There is one of a nude woman lying on the grass beside a stream. The artist attempted something very difficult in this canvas. There is a boat nearby. The woman has been bathing. She has taken brightly colored cushions from the boat and thrown them on the grass.

No one is near. She lies there, her eyes looking off into the distance. Her arms are thrown above her head.

The warm flesh is lovely against the green.

A tree nearby is much alive. It is all tree, as the woman is all woman.

At the brook's edge are some silvery stones and the boat on the river is gray.

The painter is trying to make color and light sing across his canvas as the musician tries to make sounds sing and as I try sometimes to make words sing and rattle and cry out on my pages.

And so seldom succeed.

There is this world of these artists and it is aside from the world in which much of my life is spent, but how I love to come occasionally among them as I am doing now. As I am a writer, writing of people, I must spend much of my life buried in the ordinary life of people.

But how I love to hear the sincere inquiring painter

talk of his light, his color, his masses of solids. When I go back to my own hills I shall see them in a new and more vivid way for being here in this room.

There is life in painting nowadays. As in writing prose, few enough men succeed but many are trying.

They have "since Cezanne lived," they all say (and it must be true), a new sense of color in life. The backgrounds of paintings are not dead now.

There is another painting. A cat is lying stretched out among soft, colorful cushions.

But I will not speak more of these paintings now. The painter's wife has just come into the room, looking for a workbasket she left here.

Her coming diverts my thoughts. In a nearby yard children are crying to one another with their sharp little voices. An early spring wind is racing through bare branches of the trees outside the window.

I think of the musician's and the painter's world and of my own world.

Color, light, sound, the shapes of things.

People.

To go, as I do, into the painter's world, into the world of the musician or the sculptor, is a voyage into a delightful foreign country.

In a distant part of the house I hear the voice of the painter's wife explaining something to him.

"My dear, when I spoke sharply to you, when you

were impatient for your breakfast, I was not really in a bad humor. I loved you then and I love you now."

"Well, go away, my dear. I am thinking about painting now. I am not thinking about love."

I do not think of love looking at the woman on the grass. I think of warm colors in flesh, of the strangeness and wonder of the human form.

I think of the hills of my own country and of how, sometimes, when I walk or ride among them, they are like lovely women.

I think of men ploughing in fields, of the breasts of horses as they come toward me along the furrows. I think of the sounds made by Virginia streams, rolling and tumbling over rocks.

I think of men meeting and talking, of men riding in automobiles, of lawyers, doctors, farmers, laborers.

A procession of figures floats through my mind.

I am like every one else in America. I am always wanting to do something big. Only yesterday I walked in the streets of New York thinking of a great novel I might some day write.

I wanted to be a Zola, a Hugo, a Balzac.

What nonsensical thoughts I had.

Why am I not content to be small?

GERTRUDE STEIN

An ARTICLE ABOUT Gertrude Stein, by B. F. Skinner, appeared in the *Atlantic*. Hers is automatic writing. That was the conclusion. A pretty good case was made for the conclusion, but if you think the same result can be accomplished by any one trying automatic writing, try it. If you happen to be a person of real talent, with a feeling for words, word relationships, word color, you may get something that will surprise and please you. Otherwise, you will get pure drivel. It comes to the same thing with all writing— all of us write as well as we can. What is there comes out.

Color sense is something you must be born with. The painter seeks color and, as any good painter knows, there is form in color. A half hour with nature will prove it to you. Go to a hilltop on any day when the light is waning. There is a valley spread out before you. As the light changes forms also change. The form of the spring hill covered with trees is not the same as the form of the same hill, the trees splashed with color in the fall.

Go into the woods now and begin picking up tiny bits of color. There are broken bits of tree bark, tiny stones, pieces of leaf. Hold these in your cupped hand. Let the light in slowly. See how amazingly the forms change as the light changes the color.

This matter of writing, the use of words in writing, is an odd affair. How much Miss Stein has taught all of us! Let us admit, at the beginning, that there is a confusion here. Words are used to convey thought, but there is for the prose man, as for the poet, such a thing as pure and beautiful prose. At least this may be said for the arts of painting or for music. The layman approaches these arts with a humbleness not in him when he approaches prose writing. We prosemen have both the handicap and glory of using man's speech as tools, and I have often heard sentences on the street that glow like jewels. There are critics, in this country, and I presume in all countries, who spend their lives writing about writing and who can never, by any chance, know anything about it. You can't be blamed if you are born color-blind.

When it comes to that, the same thing can be said about a good many writers.

Musicians and painters often have this attitude toward writing and in particular toward prosemen. A man like

Hemingway writes a sentence. The man can make sentences. He is one of the living writers who can.

To be sure, there is something else to writing. Writers also deal with thoughts, impulses in themselves and other men. It is possible to have a very fine mind, fine impulses, great earnestness, even profoundly to affect a civilization while writing miserably.

A musician, a composer, walking with me, spoke of his art and of my own. He said he envied me. We were standing on a bridge. "There is water flowing under the bridge," he said. "How very simple. You want your reader to know about the water. You say, 'The water runs under the bridge.' There you are."

It is simple, isn't it? A good many books are written in that spirit. As though we writers did not work always for the unnamable overtone—to be got by word color, if you please. A few so-called great writers have written without ever touching it. Moore, Melville and Turgenev had it—Borrow superlatively. These are your great writers—writers' writers. They would all have appreciated what Stein has been doing.

This nonsense about automatic writing. All good writing is, in a sense, automatic. It is and it isn't. When I am really writing, not doing as I am doing now, thinking the words out as I go, making an argument, but am really writing, it is always half automatic. There is something stored within that flows out. When you drive an automobile you are not necessarily, at the moment, thinking automobile.

As I write I am outside the world of reality. Here is a confusion many minds seem unable to get past. The world of art, of any art, is never the real world. The world of the novel or the story is not the world of reality. There is a world outside of reality being created. The object is not to be true to the world of reality but to the world outside reality. You want color—word color—that brings vitality also into that world.

In this world, when it is successfully created, everything counts. Word is laid against word as carefully, and always instinctively, as any painter would lay one color against another. Have you got it? You have or you haven't. Thinking, consciousness, will not do it. To a good many people all I am saying here will be nonsense. You have been told that Rembrandt was a great painter. Do you know why? A painter should know. You may say what you please to me about the personal character of Mr. George Moore. You may like the man, his mind or his character, or you may not, but if you tell me he was not a very great writer, in a way for example that a thousand Thomas Hardys could never be, then I am sure you know nothing of his writing.

Stein is great because she is a releaser of talent. She is a path-finder. She has been a great, a tremendous influence among writers because she has dared, in the face of ridicule and misunderstanding, to try to awaken in all of us who write a new feeling for words. She has done it.

"Take the word outside so-called 'sense' for the time if you please," she has said. "Let the word man in you come forth, dance for a time." For example, it is true of me, as I know it must be of any man who loves writing, that I have at times great difficulty in making the escape out of reality, so-called, into what is the greater reality.

It is necessary for the writer to go out and come in by path of words. The word sense has to be brought back. Color lies in the word, form in the color. There have been ages when all painting was dull and drab. Whistler was a bad painter. He had no color. If you please he had too much mind, or what he thought was mind. It took a Cezanne to bring color back. "Oh," they cried, "but he has no form. He cannot draw, *etc*." Hang the Cezanne in your room. The form will come into it. Go from the painting of Madame Cezanne to Whistler's Mother. Now see where the form is, where the drawing.

"The trouble with Stein is that she doesn't make sense."

"Whose sense?"

Wait. Stein is a revolutionist. If we ever get again a world that knows what pure writing is, the sense and form in Stein's work will come through. She also will stand as a restorer of "the word."

A MAN'S MIND*

"Assorted Essays"

An Absurd Title really for these little flashes out of a man's mind, brilliant, clear little flashes of the mind of a man at work.

But why say just mind? D. H. Lawrence never wrote just with his mind. The whole sensitive male body of the man must have tingled as he wrote. You feel man flesh in his words, nerves alive, the man smelling, tasting, seeing. He must have written often with a rush.

He had a small, not-too-strong man's body.

What life there was in it! It was male life fighting for an old thing maleness once meant.

It was sweet life, too. Women should hate to see this man die. D. H. Lawrence was one of the few clean males of literature. He was a lover. He was male.

Some one told me, one day recently, that he was dead.

"What?"

"Yes, he died."

"Why, I did not think he was ready to die yet."

* Review of a book of essays published after Lawrence's death.

87

But you can never tell when death will slip up suddenly on a man. He had been diseased, they say, a long time—a persistent physical disease eating away at him.

Himself burning, burning, a bright light in a murky time.

I think of other English writers of his day. Where are they? What one of them ever gave as this man did?

They are such a respectable lot . . . National Liberal Club . . . Something of that sort, wanting to be English gentlemen.

What has being an artist to do with being a gentleman? Lawrence knew so much, felt so much. He must have been hurt and hurt and hurt again. What did he care about being an English gentleman? Sir D. H. Lawrence. Impossible, thank God.

Now he is dead. People should begin to read him now. No one need be jealous of the man, no need now to call him dirty, ban him because he loved life so vitally that he was always wanting to touch it, put his hands on it.

Oh, thou dry-neck, here was a living man for you? Be ashamed before the life in him!

People should read Lawrence now. Young men should read him. Begin with "Assorted Essays" if you haven't begun. Read down through him.

They'll tell you "Sons and Lovers" was his best book. Don't believe it. He wrote that long ago and the man became more and more vital until he died.

You young men . . . want to know about the machine age . . . what it is doing to men . . . the way out. Here is a man who found a way out. He lived.

He returned to flesh . . . to living men and women, taking them close, loving, feeling with them. He got money into the right place too. What fine contempt in him.

Oh, thou dry-neck, here was a man! Here was a man not afraid to remain loose, fluid, alive—to the last. It couldn't have been more than two or three years before he died that he wrote "Lady Chatterley's Lover." What a clean, fine book, making everything about you clean and nice as you read.

Making people clean and nice again, as Whitman at his best did, making them again feel to you as fields and trees feel.

You'll get the same feeling from "Assorted Essays" . . . unless you also are, alas, dry-neck, in which case all of Lawrence will be just stench to you . . .

As Whitman was to the dry-necks.

As are cattle in fields, women hungering for physical love and children, men puzzled and defeated, dogs, little chicks coming out of egg shells . . . all the strange forgotten loveliness of life going on . . . in spite of dry-necks . . . all the eternal wonder of it.

I cannot write very steadily of D. H. Lawrence. I never knew the man personally, but his death, the news of it coming to me, was like a light going out at night in a cold, strange house. It left me standing against a wall in the house, feeling along the wall for the door, wanting to get out into the night and under the stars.

A country doctor told me of Lawrence's death. He is a man who has a country practice in the hills of Tennessee, and, being a lonely man, he reads a lot of books.

I had gone to see this man, this country doctor, and was spending a week with him.

We drove about the country and into the hills.

On the day when he told me of Lawrence's death we had got out of his car to take a walk in a woods.

The sun was shining. There was a cold spring wind blowing.

The leaves were just starting to unfold on some of the trees. The little red bunches of swelling, straining leaves, wanting to unfold, were like flesh.

They were like sweet flesh, such as the flesh of people might be, sweet flesh conscious of its own sweetness.

The doctor took a city newspaper, and had read it that morning while I idled in bed. In the wood, as we walked along a path, he stopped suddenly by a tree.

He made a quick motion about the trunk of the tree with his hand. The doctor has nice hands. They are all alive. He had grabbed at something.

Life, eh?

He had caught a little gray tree lizard and held it in his hand open before me. There in the palm of his hand the little gray creature sat . . . intensely alive. Its little throat throbbed and all its tiny body was a-quiver.

How nice the gray-greenish throbbing body of the lizard against the man's flesh of the doctor's hand, a hand that had released many mountain babies into the world, that had for years been touching people, healing people.

The doctor held the tiny thing in his hand and then, stooping down, released it in the path.

It ran quickly away, gray-green blending against the gray-green dead leaves under the trees.

"D. H. Lawrence is dead," the doctor said.

"What?

"I did not think he was ready to die yet."

"You can't tell about Death," the doctor said . . . "Death has its own way with men, too."

As life does.

I was asked to write a review of this little book of essays, "Assorted Essays," by D. H. Lawrence, published after his death. Review indeed! Who am I to write reviews? I can't write of the man so, I can't center on one book. The book is called "Assorted Essays," and it is a stupid title. The essays are quickly read. They are like little jewels, held in the hand as the doctor held the lizard, light playing on them. They are like a covey of quail at the edge of a field, little, feathered, trembling bundles of life, lying close in dry grass, ready to take wing and be off.

They come out of the workshop of a man . . . not a gentleman . . . an artist, really . . . one of the few prose artists of our times.

There are always little nice things happening in relation to one for whom you have love.

I have felt love for D. H. Lawrence since the first sentence of his I ever read.

A man I know, a critic, has written me a letter about the dead Lawrence—a kind of questionnaire.

"Do you think so and so?"

A row of little questions.

"I want to get him placed in relation to the whole body of English writing."

"You do, eh?"

"Three strikes. You're out."

I have thrown that critic's letter in the fire, where it deserves to be.

The book "Assorted Essays" came to me in the mail as I was going trout fishing with a man who is woods boss in a lumber camp. He is a man with big mustaches and big hands that can handle a trout rod with infinite delicacy.

I had got the book out of the Post Office.

"You read a lot, eh?" the woods boss said, seeing me put it in the door pocket of the car.

Alas, not much.

That country doctor, we both knew, would be reading ten times more books in a year.

But I read this book.

I had clambered down over rocks to a pool. I cast three times and got a trout.

The book was in my pocket and so I thought, "I'll read it here."

It was a good place. There cannot possibly be many more books left by Lawrence.

Such books are good to read by trout streams in the hills, in pine forests, in the presence of a woman loved . . .

In the presence of cornfields, perhaps.

The little book of essays stood up to it, was beautiful under that hard test.

Oh, you dry-necks!

I read some of the living little essays down there on a rock at the pool's edge and the rest in a road above, where I am now. I can hear the roar of water tumbling over rocks as I write.

I am out of paper. I did not carry much in my pocket.

In clambering up the rocks to the road I have hurt my hand. It bleeds. There is a persistent little bleeding.

It has besmeared with my own blood, some of the pages on which I write these words of Lawrence dead, to bleed no more.

Little red blotches of my blood covering the sheets on which I try to write of D. H. Lawrence, dead.

Spoiling the sheets.

Blood spoiling clean white sheets of paper.

Not quite. Blood is nice on white sheets on which a man speaks, even falteringly, of a man's man like D. H. Lawrence.

LAWRENCE
AGAIN

THE CHARM, THE WON-
der of D. H. Lawrence is just this—that you take him
or you leave him. For you he is or he is not. He's yours
or he isn't. You have a feeling that he never really cared,
not about that. I mean that he never really cared about
too much vulgar being taken. There was something for
which he did care. Caring was strong, a living impulse
in him.

He was a man absorbed and intent. What man would
not prefer to live his life so? Any man, who is a man,
would like to carry all through his life all he can carry.
*"The Now is a country to discover which, to be the
pioneer in which, I would give all thought, all memories,
all hope. My ship has but skirted the shores of that
country."*

The Now—the Present—is dark and uncertain. How
well, how cleverly, men fix up, in their minds, the past
and the future. They do not have to face immediately the
past and the future. There is time always to make up lies.

95

Not that all men necessarily want to make up lies.

The Now—the Present—is right here. It is in this room. It is like some one coming suddenly, unexpectedly, in at the door there, that door, there by my desk.

Saying, "Well, what about it?" Let them tackle the problem of the Now, as Lawrence did, try to penetrate that, go into the immediacy of the living Now. If there is darkness, let them try to penetrate and understand darkness, the strange terrible darkness of the Now. Lawrence did. Lawrence was always willing to shoot the works, to plunge.

I have never been able to read a Lawrence book without feeling something ——

His Kingship. That is what I feel.

Most of us—who live in our day—are such cave-ins. We are defeatists, lost souls. We grow smart and cynical. "Life isn't worth living," we say. Why? What sheer, hopeless nonsense.

Life—what else is there?

We humans are both too much and not enough concerned with one another. We are in a half-way stage, out of something and, we hope, into something. Individuality has gone to seed in us and we do not dare yet reach toward all life—sense of a moving pageant outside self—that might lead into a purer, finer individuality.

The glory of Lawrence is that he never gave out that kind of betraying cry against life. He never went smart-aleck. I am not taking into account, in writing of this man, some of the books that have been written about him since his death. I have looked into some of them and they do not touch him. What they do to me is to give me an interesting, or shuddering picture, of some other personality—utterly outside Lawrence. They are like the Spanish moss on a sturdy live-oak tree in the South— not a part of the tree and its life at all—living not on the tree, or with roots in the ground from which the tree came, but just floating, detached things—attaching— feeding on air.

Ever since I began to know D. H. Lawrence . . . and I have known him since he began to appear in print . . . you do not miss such a man . . . I never met him, never had any correspondence with him . . . but, from the first, I've said to myself, regarding him: "There's Kingship. There is nice clean maleness, alive again in this man."

Try to imagine D. H. Lawrence creeping through streets, taking strange women, taking another man or another woman, casually—the ultimate insult. You can't. Try to imagine him a Don Juan. You can't.

It is a thing—this clean maleness—that very few men achieve in any generation. D. H. Lawrence had it. He was born with it. He fought valiantly all of his life to hold it. I know of but one other man—at least in the arts—who in the last half-dozen generations has seemed to me to have it so clearly. I have felt the thing in only two men of our times whose work has touched me closely, and in the case of each man I have got my sense of it entirely from the work each man has done.

You get oddly the same impression of both men . . . both men sensitive and shy about the great problem every man has to face. How am I to find the woman? Can I function with her on the high fine plane of real manhood . . . an end to whoredom . . . male and female whoredom.

Recently I've read books about Lawrence: "The Letters of D. H. Lawrence"—"Apocalypse"—Murry's "Son of Woman," and Catherine Carswell's "The Savage Pilgrimage." I've read Mabel Dodge Luhan's "Lorenzo in Taos."

Now I would like, here, to say something about D. H. Lawrence's Kingship, the whole notion of Kingship in men—in the male—the Kingship D. H. Lawrence represented for me so perfectly.

To me it is like this . . . Nowadays, for all of us I think, there is a choice to be made. Lawrence was a man of talent. His talent wasn't steady, a sure balanced thing. It was fine, high, and delicate, that talent of his. He had to carry it. He knew it. He wasn't afraid to try. Suppose you had to carry a cup, full to the brim with delicate wine . . . yourself bound by some law of your being always to try never to spill or waste a drop of it but to carry it forward during your life, through the modern world.

What time have you to be saying . . . "Is life worth living,". . . that sort of thing?

Carrying it through the life of a young coal miner.

Through coal mining towns.

In publishers' houses.

To literary parties.

To socialistic meetings.

You know what modern life is like. D. H. Lawrence couldn't stay hidden away. He always wanted, I dare say, to go through life walking in quiet forests, in fields, in the quieter back streets of little towns, but the man was too arresting. There was too much male force in him. He always attracted others. They came flocking to him in crowds, men and women.

I dare say he muddled it with a few women himself. He said he did.

He never went whoring with one of them. Let me try to say a word now about the wine Lawrence was always trying to carry in the cup. It was dark, rich, and fragrant. It was the essence of manhood. It was something he wanted to give to a woman. It has come to be the style now—men without women—women without men . . . an impotent generation, talking big out of its impotence.

They would—the impotent ones—turn and shout at this man—carrying, as he always did, the essence of that strange thing, manhood, through a world that doesn't, just now, accept the often terrifying implications of manhood—or womanhood—they would turn and shout the word impotence at Lawrence.

You will see what I am driving at. Let us go on to the other implication of the man—his talent.

I think, and have always thought, that is what talent is . . . it's manhood . . . the essence of manhood . . . masculinity if you please. I admit that I often see a woman carrying it, the appearance of it. It is all right with me. I am glad for talent wherever it appears.

It seems to me there are and have always been two basic impulses in life. To do. To be. Am I being arbitrary in calling them male and female impulses?

Talent implies always one definite thing—a challenge.

The challenge is rather terrific just now, for the man of our times.

I think it is like this . . . manhood that finds its full fruition only in work, and womanhood that comes to full bloom only in physical life—in the reproduction of physical life—both these qualities, when they appear fully and richly in an individual, imply also a rich full flowering of individuality.

That means, if it means anything, Kingship and Queenship. In myself, absolute unquestioned Kingship—or Queenship. Others may question it if they will but I, if I am the man carrying the wine, spoken of above . . . it will not do for me to question.

If I have it—the thing I am here speaking of . . . I admit it is seldom understood . . . it arouses hatred . . . if I have it I should be singing songs to myself.

Having it, I know, or should know, the intense preciousness of my own life. Knowing introduces me to all life, in animals, in trees, in grasses, in the sea. Who could make you feel an animal or a tree or a flower as could D. H. Lawrence?

He knew it—in its essence—the fine wine he carried through life.

We talk much nowadays of the giving up of individuality. We have begun to say now that there is a new world born. I think it is true. The day of the old individuality has passed. We men, of our day, strive to give up individuality. We want to give it up.

It is right that we should. Why?

Here is where the contradiction comes in . . . the paradox that always rules all life. I hope I may for once say clearly what is in my mind. If you haven't talent, manliness, masculinity, or womanhood—the essence of womanhood—obviously a thing as beautiful as masculinity—then you can't give. You can't spend what you haven't got. There's your tragedy.

If you haven't a thing you can't give it. By giving you get. It is a simple enough old truth. Don't be foolish. All men want to give. What I am saying here all men know.

If you haven't to give and try to give—as you do—as all of us do—then you give always, not having to give, apologetically, hesitatingly, shamefully. You botch it. You can't help botching it. What mature man has not tried to give to some woman when he wasn't rich with giving? What woman hasn't done it? Let us confess. It is what is the matter with most of us now. There is the reason so many of us nowadays go around saying that life isn't worth living.

If I, in my own self, cannot give, having lost, because of cowardly denial of the import of manhood, or woman-hood, in myself, it is obviously the easier way out to cry out against life.

Sing the song of life again.

Kings and Queens be born again.

I think that D. H. Lawrence was one man in our times who spent his life . . . a high, feverish, eager life . . . a life that should make the rest of us ashamed . . . he spent it running with the cup, offering it to the lips of others. He had to find some one rich to receive. It may also sound a bit mystic and unclear, what I am trying to say, but it really isn't. Most men . . . and women . . . will understand well enough. You have to give up individuality to get it. There is nothing in the world you get except by giving. It is the great lesson that over and over, like children, we have to keep trying to learn. D. H. Lawrence began life as a school teacher. He always was, as are all men of talent, a teacher. He was a revolutionist—a giver. I have said it before and I say it again that I believe that D. H. Lawrence . . . was also, all his life, one of the most truly male men of our times.

MARGARET ANDERSON:
REAL — UNREAL

So you too, Margaret Anderson, have written a book . . . "My Thirty Years' War."

But Margaret, you are yourself a character in a book. You are not real. No one ever thought you were real. You are, have always been, something that comes into other lives. You are not woman. You are not man. You know little enough of the rest of us. What do we know of you?

Well, I dare say you eat. You sleep. I know that you wear clothes, gorgeously lovely clothes. Words flow from you. There are some two hundred seventy-four pages of words gathered together here, in this book you have put out for us to read. Speaking as one man, I read it, Margaret, with extreme delight. At the very end, you have signed it:

Tancerville 1929   Paris 1929.

It was early morning when I came to that and, looking at the words, I could not help wondering if you were at Tancerville.

Is it a place? Are you walking about there? Is it by the sea? Are you the splendid creature you were when I saw you last in New York? Do you occasionally run up to Paris as years ago you took the *Little Review* away from us, in Chicago, and took it to New York, not, as you said when we asked you because you specially needed New York?

You felt New York needed you. Now New York has seen you and California and Paris and God knows how many other places. There is your picture, by Man Ray, at the front of the book. You would have the best man obtainable to do the picture. God bless you for that.

What a cloud of people! James Joyce, Otto Kahn, Gertrude Stein, Mary Garden.

Ernest Hemingway, Aldous Huxley, Pablo Picasso . . . so he looks like that, eh?

Ben Hecht, Emma Goldman, noisy old Ben Reitman. A thousand people, let us say, mentioned in the pages of this book. I have not counted. There must be tens of thousands of other lives, people whose names you have not mentioned, but whose lives have touched your life. It was night and I was at my farmhouse in the country when I read your book. I read it with a sort of breathless rush, as it is written, as you used to talk. My room, in which I work and sleep, became filled with people as I read. Faces peered out at me from walls. There is a little stream comes down from the mountains and past my farmhouse door. It flows under my bedroom window. At night the sound of it, falling down over rocks, becomes louder and louder. There is a little wooden bridge coming over the stream from a road.

And so last night I read your book, not wanting to sleep, wanting to hear your voice again, wanting the rush of words from you, wanting to feel again your beautiful belief in unreality. Oh, thou unreal creature!

Did you know, Margaret, that I loved you, that a thousand men, a thousand women have loved you?

The sound of the stream below my window grew louder and louder as I read. I did not read critically. Why should I have done that, to you? Thank God you are not a literary man, or woman. You are yourself. You have as much right to talk in the pages of this book as a bird has to sing in the apple tree by my window here. A man does not write musical criticism when a bird comes thus, to sing or to chatter.

The sound of the stream below my window grew louder and louder in the night, your book being in my hand, being propped up among pillows. The sounds became confused in my mind. I put down the book for a moment.

There was the tread of heavy feet on the bridge that crosses the stream. Carl Sandburg tramped over the bridge. Theodore Dreiser came. There was the soft sound of a woman's feet. Many feet came thus over a bridge, across the floor of a farmhouse kitchen and up a stairway to my room.

People, men and women, crowded into my room.

Why, I am confused about this book. I read it in the night. How many of the people, conjured up thus by its pages, people who came into my room last night, were actually mentioned in the pages of the book? I do not know. I cannot remember. It is morning now and as I sit writing to you of the book, I have a headache. My head is too full of people and I have not slept.

I remember a young woman in Chicago. Let's not use names. Let's call her Ted. She lived where I lived in Chicago, when you were in the first flush of your youth there. You will remember the place, up Cass Street from the Loop—an old brick house. Max used to come there, and Harriet and Mary and Tennessee Mitchell and Ben and Carl and others. I don't remember that you ever came, but you knew them all and they knew and loved you.

So here was this Ted, one of the unnamed ones. She was short and fat and wanted, more than anything else, I imagine, to be a man. She used to come home from some place where she was employed down in the Chicago Loop, and put on men's overalls. She was wanting men's clothes to wear and could only afford overalls. Every one in that house was always broke.

The point is that I found her one evening on the stairs

in that house. She had on the overalls, her great breasts making them stick out absurdly in front. She sat thus, huddled up on the stairs in a kind of half darkness, her face in her hands, her hair falling over her hands.

She was crying about you. She told me that.

Why, she couldn't explain.

She wasn't in love. I asked her about that. She had been somewhere and had seen you and she said you gave her a feeling about everybody she had never had before. It is a feeling that comes and goes.

Let's admit that. We are an outlaw people. Those of us who write words, tramp the boards of the stage, spread paint on canvas, chip, carve, hammer, trying to reach into unreality through the real, do not belong.

There is the world about us and it is not our world. We never made it. It keeps saying to us . . . "You must have bread and clothes. Come to terms, then."

We do come to terms. In America we are doing it all the time. Among ourselves we quarrel and fight. We say bitter, biting things of each other. America is a place gone mad with publicity. The outside world, the world of reality in which we are compelled, it seems, to live, the world your mother wanted you to live in . . . you have been cruel enough to her, God knows . . . drags us down constantly out of the unreal into the real.

There should be a kind of brotherhood of the unreal.

We of the unreal should stand always shoulder to shoulder, but we do not do it, cannot do it.

The unreal world fades constantly and the real world is always here. We are filled with petty jealousies. To-day some one man or woman, from among us, is in the public eye.

The newspaper and the critic have taken up such a one. There he is. He is being praised on all sides. Money rolls in to him. Now, in the real world, he is receiving the applause of the masses.

Tomorrow it will be transferred from him to another. He will have a hard struggle to get back again into our world, into the world of unreality.

None of the others of us helps him much.

You would.

And there are all sorts of borderline cases. You cannot say definitely . . . "This one belongs in here, that one does not belong." I suppose that at moments all people come in and out. How else could you have run the *Little Review* in Chicago? Why did fat business men give you checks to keep your crazy little magazine afloat, why didn't the real-estate man throw you out of that apartment that looked over the lake . . . (don't tell me you paid your rent. I know better) . . . why was the printer so patient with you? He was a poor man and never got his money. I know he never did.

Why didn't you stay in America, in Chicago? Why did you go to France, to Tancerville?

Well, it is all right. It is no one's business what you do.

In Chicago, when you came there, you were most needed. You came. You appeared out of the most absurd of all possible places. I think it was Floyd Dell who first told me of you. "She exists," he said; "a woman who will start a magazine here."

"It will be a free magazine," he said.

Of course, I didn't believe. I was working in an advertising agency, writing advertisements. How can a man doing that believe anything? I began to ask questions. "Has she any money? Where is she?"

"She is being literary editor of some kind of church magazine. No, she hasn't any money.

"She will do it though."

But she will be taken up by some particular crowd here. If she can get the money. That is what will happen.

"You say she is a beautiful woman. Some man will give her the money."

"The magazine if it is started will represent some movement. It will take up the cause of the realists, or the romanticists, or the humanists. We have all become modernists. It will be a modernists' magazine."

"Wait and see," Floyd said.

And so I did wait and see. I saw men and women of our unreal world become real to each other for a time.

I saw men and women standing together. I saw belief springing up. I saw men of my own real-unreal world all drawn together.

I never believed you had much sense of people, Margaret Anderson. In this book of yours when you pass judgment on people you are absurd. You always were absurd, anyway. What difference does that make?

You gave a lot of queer, isolated people a quick and sudden sense of each other. Something started. You walked about, being personally beautiful, as I dare say you are now. You talked with a quick rush of words. You walked in a certain way.

None of the men you gathered about you tried to get you as his own woman, as his own individual woman. It would have been absurd to think of that.

We were all of us sunk down into the muddle of life, real life, God knows. We were falling in love. Two of us men were fighting over some woman. We were full of jealousies and hatreds. Women were hating each other. There had been a dozen little petty groups started.

You got us all together. We came to you. We worked for you. Cæsar swept out your office. He ran your errands. Harriet worked. Jane worked. Business men gave you money. I dare say all kinds of people gave you clothes and flowers. Why not?

You inspired love and devotion. You weren't after anything. You never did push yourself forward. You didn't have to. You had but to walk through the streets, through a hotel lobby. Wherever you went men's eyes followed you, women's eyes followed you. Women were not jealous of you. Men did not look at you with greasy eyes.

You were not like the rest of us, struggling down there in the Chicago mud, going constantly falteringly, in and out of our unreal world. You were unreal. You were a character in a play. You were a novel or a painting come to life.

You started the *Little Review.* There were other sudden outbursts of flame everywhere. The old *Masses* got started, the *Seven Arts*, the new *Dial*, with Gilbert Seldes as editor . . . (there was an editor for you) . . . the *Double Dealer* down at New Orleans. It was a rich time. You were at the bottom of it all.

You succeeded. You were made to live always in an unreal world. You have written a book. You are at Tancerville. I insist upon the sea and the white sand. There are people there. You walk up and down before them as once you walked the streets of Chicago, when the *Little Review* was getting started. People look at you. You do not touch their real lives, do not want to.

Why, Margaret, you have not written a book. This is not a book. It is a flash-back of yourself. It is charming, Margaret, as you are charming, will always be charming. You are at Tancerville and you walk on the white beach and people look at you and then you pass. You pass and you remain. We thank you, Margaret, for this little visit to us. I personally thank you for a night of faces and of footsteps on my stairs. You have brought back other days and they were good days. You made them good days while you stayed with us.

PAUL

There are many critics who grow famous by the road of bitterness. Make it a rule. Say that everything is rotten. You will, almost always, be right.

Not that bitterness is not also a good tool with which to work.

There are, however, critics who also lift up. It is all very well occasionally to do something good, but no piece of work you can do really comes to life until another knows it is good.

And there is a sense in which the true criticism can do a thing even nobler than the finest creation. It will be less self-centered.

But pshaw . . . no man is a fine critic who is not, first of all, a creative man.

An alert supersensitive man, round and alive. Once I called him "the well-dressed man of American letters." It was in an article in which I talked of four Americans —Ring Lardner, Gertrude Stein, Sinclair Lewis and Paul

Rosenfeld. I had, perhaps for some malicious reason, great delight in grouping them. J imagined the four together, say in a cabin on a mountain, in a snowstorm. All of this not in my article, which was quite dignified, but in fancy. I saw them in the room, staring at each other. A delicious thought came to me. It was that Paul and Ring would have quickly found a basis for understanding. I can imagine them withdrawing to a corner of the room to talk.

There is no fire in the room. A storm is raging outside. It is bitterly cold.

Gertrude Stein and Sinclair Lewis are left to talk together. It is bitterly cold.

After I had written of Paul, calling him the well-dressed man of American letters, I went to Margaret Anderson.

She was then running the *Little Review*.

She and Jane Heap were sitting in a room. There was an outburst when I came in. "Well-dressed," they both cried. "Oh, Sherwood, Sherwood!"

At that time they were in the midst of the great Joyce obsession. Joyce was the end and he was the beginning. I had it, too. In me the attack was not so violent. It had not quite robbed me of my reason.

To me Paul was, in truth, the well-dressed one. He was one who cared about the word. In my own struggles with the word, he was the one who had been most helpful.

To me he was the man, among all our critics, most sensitive, most creatively alive.

To every writer there comes a certain experience. There are few writers—of the real sort, of the men who write day after day for years, thousands of words put down, gallons of ink poured forth—who do not now and then hit the mark.

There is a certain experience, delicious when it first comes.

"There. I have done it."

There is conviction. There is humbleness. There is pride.

"This is what I have been wanting, waiting for."

"There is this bit of work done—large or small, about which there can be no question."

The man jumps up from his desk. He walks up and down the room.

"Aha! There."

"They can all go to hell now," he cries.

"Aha! That time I had a real hop on my fast one."

The man is in a curiously humble, curiously proud sort of ecstasy. "I do not care who knows it. To me now it does not matter if no one knows. At last, this once, I have done it."

"I do not care." What rot. How deeply he does care.

And now look out. This is where your critics will fail

you. If, at the moment mentioned above, you were curiously clean, they will call you dirty. If you were clear, they will call you muddled.

It is at this moment, in the life of the writer, the painter, the maker of music, that Paul Rosenfeld arrives.

"Aha! And so there is this man who really cares."

It is a curious, an invaluable gift. It is something unexpected. I do not believe that there can come, in the life of any living writer, maker of music, painter, such a moment as that suggested above without Paul Rosenfeld's knowing.

And how well-dressed he is about it all. Why, he does not even patronize you. A year later you will not get a note from him. "A year ago I did something for you. Now you do something for me."

There is something bitter in him. One night, during the World War, I went with him to a concert. We arrived somewhat early and went to sit in a row of empty seats. The theater began to fill.

Presently a woman arrived. She had a seat near us but when she saw us sitting there, she drew back. There was a curious look in her eyes. Oh, with what contempt she looked at us. Throwing back her shoulders she marched away into the darkness at the back of the theater.

I looked at Paul with amazement. I had never seen the woman before. "Is it you?" I asked. "Yes," he said. There was a shy little smile on his lips.

"And what did you do?"

"Oh, nothing," he said.

The woman was the president of some women's society whose purpose it is to encourage good music. There are a good many such societies—the Association for the Advancement of This or That.

Morals, the Conduct of Children, the Works of Artists.

The Association for Making Cheerful and Homelike Hotel Rooms.

All of this was during or immediately after the World War. Now I remember that my friend Paul was a soldier in the World War. I have heard a tale of World War soldiers in hospitals. There were associations of women to nurse them. Some one told me that in the hospitals the soldiers used to hang signs on their beds. "Please, please, do not nurse me today."

As for the lady in the theater at the concert. It had been reported that the Germans during the war used the bodies of the dead for commercial purposes, and Paul had written of the matter in some magazine. He had mentioned the name of the association of which the rich and prominent woman who fled from us in the theater was president. "What of it?" Paul had said. He said he did not know whether or not the Germans had used the bodies of soldiers for commercial purposes. "This association of ladies has been doing it for years," he had written.

TO JASPER DEETER:
A LETTER

DEAR JAP:

I find that I cannot make the picture of you I have had in mind. It seems to me at once that what you have done at your Hedgerow Theatre, near Philadelphia, is to make the theater a way of life.

You have in that way beat the theater to something.

I imagine you going over there to what is now the Hedgerow—wanting something for yourself—you having been an actor in the New York theater.

I think that in talking to you I never told you that, long before I knew you as a friend, I saw you as an actor. It was in one of Eugene O'Neill's plays, "The Emperor Jones." You were the scrubby little Englishman, dirty of soul, cast down among the Negroes, in the Negro empire the American ex-pullman-car porter had set up.

Hating the damn nigger—kowtowing to him—planning to do him up.

A performance, beautifully and intelligently done—so that it sticks in my mind yet—much more than the performance of whatever actor it was who on that night did the emperor.

But this is not a letter to boost your own ego. I hope it may be a letter from a friend to a friend expressing something of what I feel about you—and your Hedgerow Theatre.

The theater in the old stone building there, on a side road, rather hard to find—I got lost several times trying to find it and you.

I had written a play and was puzzled thinking of the managers, my collaborator—others I had talked to about the play.

But, Jasper Deeter, let me try to get to something your theater made me feel.

I have seen performances of plays in your theater—done by your group of players that were not so slick. There were points in the play not well made.

God knows I have seen, in the New York theater, actors and more actors, who would score every point, get every laugh, hold out, stretch to the limit, every shade of the dramatic situation devised.

After such a show the audience goes out of a theater. "What a grand actor she is."

"What a show."

"It was a swell show."

"I thought he was swell."

Etc., etc., etc., etc. Poor theater! Poor actors! Poor play makers!

It is for them alone—the play goers—so often stupid enough people—middle-aged business men, out with their loves—wanting their minds taken off losses in The Street.

Fat women—wives of the well-to-do.

For godsake, play makers, directors, actors, do not by any chance give them in the theater anything at all close to the actuality of living, everyday living.

Remember the theater is so and so.

Do not make them think

Forever and Forever!

No! No!

Will it always go on? There are all of these other workers—the play makers. It must be rather disheartening for them too. "I cannot do what I want to do in the theater. I will go to 'the coast,' to the movies—make some money."

Money, money, money.

"It's money makes the mare go." As though money ever solved anything.

"Aha—'the coast'—a thousand a week."

"Sure, I shall write tripe out there but afterwards, with my pockets full of money, I shall come away. With my pockets full of movie money I shall walk through the streets of American towns and cities.

"I shall see life whole. Look, I have all of this money in my pockets. With so much money in my pockets how can I fail to see life whole?"

But did I not say I would go back to you, and your theater? I see you then as a young actor, before you went to Hedgerow, in Broadway plays.

You have done a part like that of the dirty-souled Englishman, in O'Neill's "Emperor Jones."

Now, the life of the actor for you. There is a new play being cast. Why, there is Jasper Deeter. He does these dirty little rotters very, very well!

And so on and on— Your own feeling of desperation sometimes. "But I am not just that." Because you may have done one thing well to be compelled to do it, over and over.

For well enough I know that there is, must be, a relationship between the actor and his parts.

The parts gradually but surely making the man—as "the coast" must inevitably remake every man who goes there to work—fools to think it does not—the actor made and remade constantly by the parts he plays just as he must always be making the parts.

Do I not know? I am a story-teller. Do you not think that I know that I am remade by every story I write? I would be a fool not to know. I do not want just one life. I want a thousand lives. I am a writer. Is that more honorable than being an actor? It is not.

But I, the writer, am also a shrewd enough man to know that, now—in our time—nothing can be done on the grand scale. "Be little." I constantly say to myself, "Be content to be little." It has become a kind of song in me.

Not that there is any special nobility in me. It is but shrewdness. Am I to make my shirt stink with sweat because this or that man or woman has written a book that sells fifty or a hundred thousand copies—because he has suddenly become famous?

Fifty thousand copies sold to whom?

There never were that many intelligent, discriminating people in the world.

How many people know anything about the theater— or my own beautiful art—the art of the prose writer?

Or care?

Alas, in this matter, my feelings are involved. Like you, I am a moral man.

You told me once of how you, as a younger man, a young actor, kept a pair of roller skates in the New York theater where you were playing and of how, after your evening's work was done, you went out of the theater by a back alleyway and put on the skates. There would have been this other thing—the typical New York audience, at a successful play, going out at the front of the playhouse.

And you, with your skates on—skating rapidly through

the traffic, bareheaded. "I was just a nut," you said, laughing, when you told me that. Yes, I know, wanting the clean fresh night air, wanting winds to blow on you.

Skating thus sometimes, on and on, for hours at a time—wanting.

Aha!

Past dark silent night houses—through streets.

People living in houses, in apartments.

". . . the theater should be so and so—it should be . . ."

Yes, I know. I have myself been so, running and walking sometimes for hours late at night through the sleeping streets of American towns.

You would in some way have got the idea—belief ——

"People really want to act. It is a dominant, a real feeling in people.

"There is a way, some way, by which actors may find, in acting, a way of life."

You would have tried things—outside the big theaters. I know something about that too.

Proletarian art.

Lift up the laboring masses.

Men, leaders of this or that radical movement telling you how to do it.

And so, at last, I come to your own theater.

Well, no—not your own. I do not know the history of your Hedgerow, its organization.

There would have been no money.

People coming in with you . . . old men, young men, girls, women.

The man who drives a gasoline truck.

The automobile salesman.

We'll begin—here. These people will sell us this building on time.

"If you can make a living outside—do that."

"If not, come here."

"We will in some way eat."

"At any rate we will share what comes in."

At first no doubt, often a fifty, a hundred dollar week.

In this matter of plays—the successful big ones telling me—the play makers, directors, managers.

"We must have four thousand a week. We cannot keep a play on that does not pull in four thousand" (oh, holy and devout sum) "a week."

And then the people you must have got in—the actors, I mean.

Confusion.

"Is he trying to gyp us?"

I remember that you told me once—"there is less of that, the skepticism, than you would think."

Reinforcing one of my own old beliefs—always being lost.

And again regained—that people really want belief.

To be sure, you will constantly be losing some of your people.

There are people who will never be able to stand the régime of that life you and your group lead.

The way you sometimes beat them, pound it into them. I can hear your voice calling to an actor, "No! No! That can't be the way you feel the lines, the literature. Let it come into you, get hold of you. Let loose your own feeling for once."

What might seem to an outsider the slave-like life you and the others live down there—the all-night rehearsals —your own never-tired voice—"we are being pretty rotten, boys and girls, but let's keep on.

"You say you want to be an actor. Come on, then! Act!"

"This part you are trying to do . . . for godsake, man . . . the writer was not a dub. He really meant to say something. Please, please, let yourself understand what he is trying to say."

Once, one night, I heard you—your voice not tired— it a little rasping, exasperated—(this at four in the morning) beginning again, slowly, paiently ——

"This is what the man, who wrote this part, was trying to get said."

"God knows . . . he may be a damn fool. I don't know . . ."

"We, all of us, wouldn't have tried to do his play unless we had all thought it worth doing."

"Listen! The damnfool play writer may be trying to say something."

"We have all agreed we want to do his play . . ."

"I wouldn't have any of you think that, as an actor, I take off my hat to any play writer ——"

"But."

Or again—"We actors are a special tribe. You know that. When we become actors, we agree now and then, to throw our own personalities away."

"Not that we, as actors, agree entirely to throw life away . . ."

"They have asked that of us too often."

This being a lame enough attempt at a picture of you, putting one of your actors on the pan.

And they take it? They like it? Bless them all. I myself have got humble before the actors you have made, that you are making.

. . . A limited enough group . . .

. . . Knowing, through your own intelligence and the intelligence you constantly arouse in them . . .

. . . Being, as I have said, what they are . . .

. . . Sometimes insurance agents, sweet enough young girls . . .

. . . Older men and women who came to you tired until you taught them not to be tired . . .

My seeing this, looking at you . . .

. . . as though you were always asserting something . . . often so dead in us Americans but so real in us . . .

. . . our American hunger for life.

Sometimes you have made me feel that we Americans might yet, in spite of hell and high water, be a people.

For they do join you, cling, stick to you.

You're something. I wonder what. Are you going to be, in the end, a maker of great actors?

Probably not.

But what then?

I think I know.

You are an educator—one of the few we have had in the American scene, in the American theater.

Does it satisfy you? I should think it might. Our theater, which should be an educational force, has been lying down on the job long enough.

SHERWOOD ANDERSON